Contemporary HOME PLANS

GARLINGHOUSE

Library of Congress No: 92-74944

ISBN: 0-938708-43-0

Submit all Canadian plan orders to:

The Garlinghouse Company
20 Cedar Street North
Kitchener, Ontario N2H 2WB
Canadians Orders only: 1-800-561-4169
Fax #: 1-519-743-1282
Customer Service #: 1-519-743-4169

TABLE OF CONTENTS

Photography by John Ehrenclou

No. 10581

*D*ramatic Two-Story Foyer

Bring the great outdoors inside in this luxurious four bedroom, three bath home. Enter the dramatic two-story foyer from the three-car garage or the double front doors. The living area is perfect for entertaining. Parlor, formal dining room, kitchen, breakfast room and living room revolve around a central staircase. You can spend your outdoor hours on the deck off the breakfast room, or screened porch off the living room. Two bedrooms, including the master suite with walk-in closet, two baths and a laundry room complete the first floor. Upstairs, the balcony overlooks the foyer and leads to two more bedrooms and a full bath.

First floor — 1,916 sq. ft.
Second floor — 740 sq. ft.
Basement — 1,916 sq. ft.
Screened Porch — 192 sq. ft.
Garage — 814 sq. ft.

Total living area — 2,656 sq. ft.

No. 10581

A Karl Kreeger Design

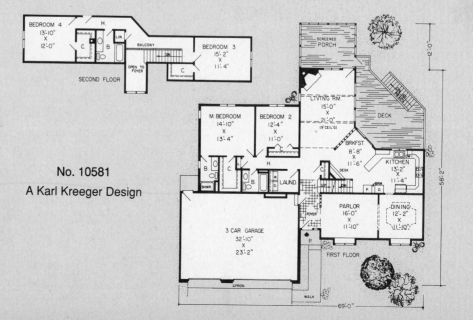

No. 20302

The wood detailing that radiates from the half round window of this inviting family home hints at the sunny atmosphere you'll find inside. Walking through the vestibule past the formal and family dining rooms, you'll encounter a two-way fireplace that warms the living and family rooms at the rear of the house. Notice the double sliders that link both rooms to a massive rear deck, and the pass-through convenience afforded by the U-shaped kitchen. Tucked behind the garage for privacy, the first-floor master suite features a skylit bath with double vanities and a luxurious spa tub. And, upstairs, three bedrooms open to a skylit lounge with a bird's eye view of the family room.

First floor — 1,510 sq. ft.
Second floor — 820 sq. ft.
Basement — 1,284 sq. ft.
Garage — 430 sq. ft.

Total living area — 2,330 sq. ft.

Photography by John Ehrenclou

S'unny and Spacious

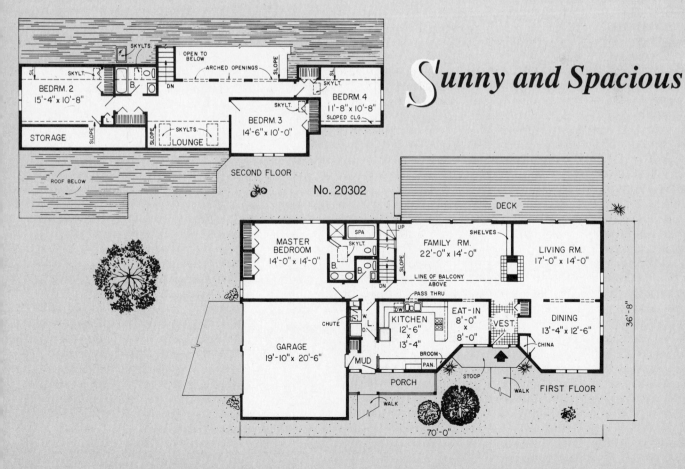

No. 20302

SECOND FLOOR

BEDRM. 2
15'-4" x 10'-8"

STORAGE

SKYLTS.

OPEN TO BELOW

ARCHED OPENINGS

SKYLT.

DN

LOUNGE SKYLTS

SLOPE

BEDRM. 3
14'-6" x 10'-0"

BEDRM. 4
11'-8" x 10'-8"
SLOPED CLG.

ROOF BELOW

FIRST FLOOR

MASTER BEDROOM
14'-0" x 14'-0"

SPA

SKYLT.

DECK

FAMILY RM.
22'-0" x 14'-0"

SHELVES

LIVING RM.
17'-0" x 14'-0"

LINE OF BALCONY ABOVE

PASS THRU

UP

SLOPE

DN

GARAGE
19'-10" x 20'-6"

CHUTE

KITCHEN
12'-6" x 13'-4"

EAT-IN
8'-0" x 8'-0"

VEST.

DINING
13'-4" x 12'-6"

CHINA

MUD

PORCH

BROOM

PAN.

STOOP

WALK

WALK

70'-0"

36'-8"

Hillside Haven

Features Solarium

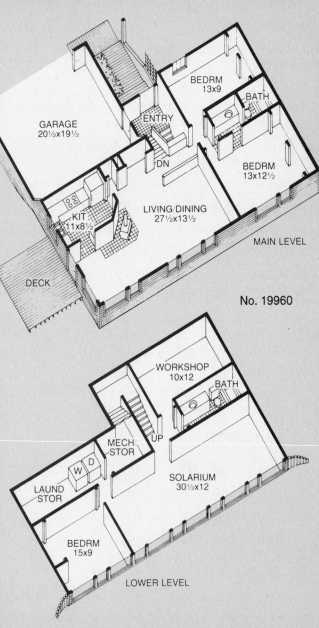

GARAGE
20½x19½

ENTRY

DN

BEDRM
13x9

BATH

BEDRM
13x12½

KIT
11x8½

LIVING/DINING
27½x13½

DECK

MAIN LEVEL

No. 19960

WORKSHOP
10x12

BATH

MECH
STOR

UP

LAUND
STOR

W D

SOLARIUM
30½x12

BEDRM
15x9

LOWER LEVEL

No. 19960

This wide-open charmer offers comfortable living for a hillside location. Step up from the entry to an attractive living and dining room combination warmed by a coal or wood stove and lots of windows. The angular wall behind the stove creates an interesting shape in the living room, and in the handy kitchen on its other side. A short hall off the entry leads to two bedrooms, each with a huge closet, and a compartmentalized full bath. On the lower level, you'll find a spacious solarium, a third bedroom, another full bath, and a handy home workshop.

Upper level — 1,064 sq. ft.
Lower level — 1,064 sq. ft.
Garage — 420 sq. ft.

Total living area — 2,128 sq. ft.

Photography by John Ehrenclou

*G*reenhouse Entrance
Accents Two-Story Berm

No. 10541

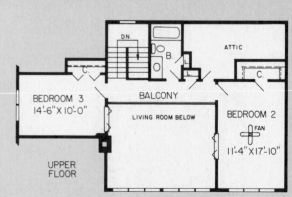

BEDROOM 3
14'-6"X10'-0"

BALCONY

LIVING ROOM BELOW

DN.

B.

C.

ATTIC

C.

FAN

BEDROOM 2
11'-4"X17'-10"

UPPER
FLOOR

Greenhouse entry into a spacious living area provides a bit of elegance as well as practicality for the energy-wise family. Both the living room and the master bedroom are furnished with ceiling fans and a heat-circulating stove. The second floor balcony, which connects bedrooms two and three upstairs, overlooks the living room. Two full baths and a powder room provide ample space for family and guests. Lots of closet space and a large utility room are features everyone appreciates.

Main floor — 1,474 sq. ft.
Upper floor — 1,044 sq. ft.
Garage — 616 sq. ft.

Total living area — 2,518 sq. ft.

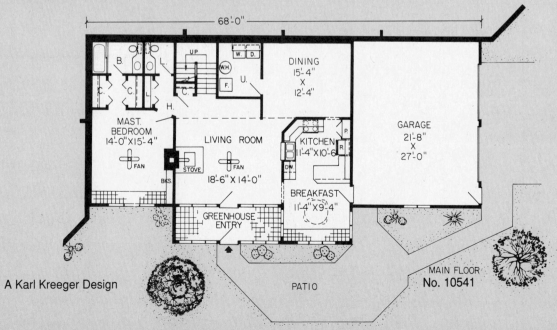

A Karl Kreeger Design

MAIN FLOOR
No. 10541

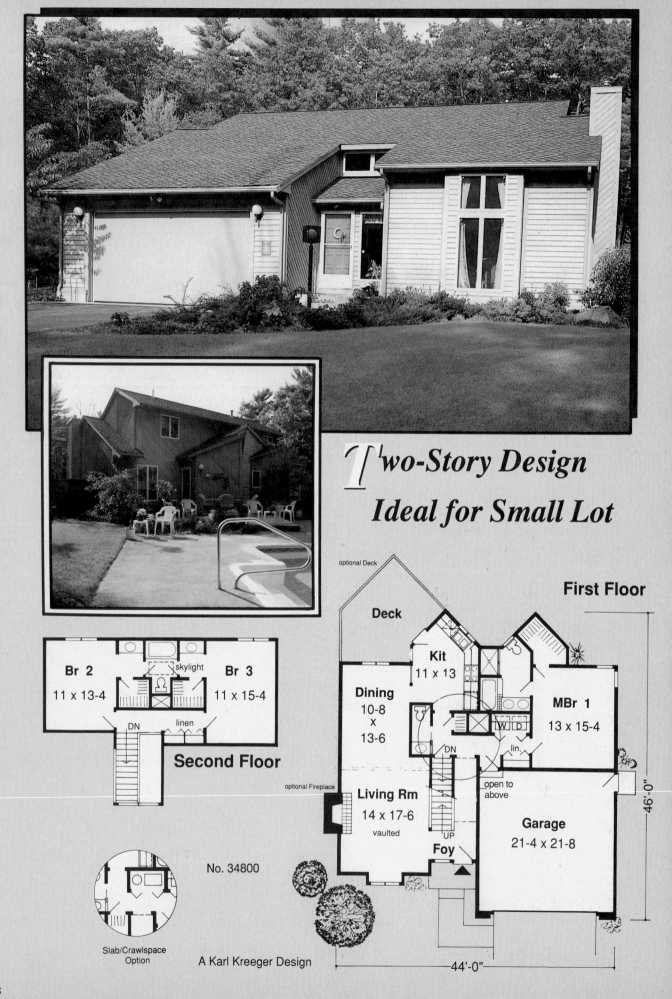

T'wo-Story Design
Ideal for Small Lot

First Floor

optional Deck

Deck

Kit
11 x 13

Dining
10-8
x
13-6

MBr 1
13 x 15-4

W D

lin.

Second Floor

Br 2
11 x 13-4

skylight

Br 3
11 x 15-4

DN

linen

DN

open to above

optional Fireplace

Living Rm
14 x 17-6
vaulted

UP

Garage
21-4 x 21-8

Foy

46'-0"

44'-0"

No. 34800

Slab/Crawlspace
Option

A Karl Kreeger Design

Photography by John Ehrenclou

On the second floor of this well-arranged home are two bedrooms which flank a bath that is illuminated by a skylight. Adjacent to the bath are individual dressing areas each with its own basin and large walk-in closet. The interesting angles incorporated into the plan of the first floor create extra space in the master suite. The living room has a sloped-ceiling and a fireplace with tile hearth. The angular kitchen includes a pantry, space for a dinette set, and direct access to the rear deck. Other features include a half-bath on the first floor, a conveniently located laundry, and an inviting two-story foyer.

First floor — 1,187 sq. ft.
Second floor — 597 sq. ft.
Basement — 1,169 sq. ft.
Garage — 484 sq. ft.

Total living area — 1,784 sq. ft.

DECK

KITCHEN
11'-4" X 13'-4"

DINING ROOM
11'-10" X 13'-8"

B.

DRESSING

C.

MASTER
BEDROOM
12'-10" X 15'-4"

B.

W. D.

H.

LIVING ROOM
16'-6" X 15'-4"

UP
DN

FOYER

C.

BEDROOM #3
10'-11" X 11'-10"

C.

BEDROOM #2
10'-7" X 13'-4"

C.

S.

ROOF

W. UP

DRIVE

No. 10524

49'-0"
UPPER FLOOR PLAN

30'-0"

FAMILY ROOM
23'-4" X 13'-2"

B.

C.

F.

BEDROOM #4
12'-8" X 13'-2"

H.

BASEMENT
23'-4" X 15'-6"

DN UP

2-CAR GARAGE
24'-0" X 21'-2"

36'-4"

DRIVE

LOWER FLOOR PLAN

*S*plit-level Made

for Growing Family

A Karl Kreeger Design

No. 10524

The entry-level living room features a fireplace and, just a few steps up, a dining room which overlooks the living room and adjoins the kitchen. The efficient kitchen features an eat-in space and sliding door access to the deck. Three bedrooms, two baths, and a convenient laundry room comprise the rest of the upper floor. The fourth bedroom, with its own bath, could be used as a guest room or to give more privacy to the teenager in the family. There's also a cozy family room and plenty of storage in the basement.

Upper floor — 1,470 sq. ft.
Lower floor — 711 sq. ft.
Basement — 392 sq. ft.
Garage — 563 sq. ft.

Total living area — 2,181 sq. ft.

Photography by John Ehrenclou

Photography by Jeff Grant

*E*nticing
Angles...

From every angle this two-story house has a special allure. Thrusting roof lines echoed in the siding pattern creates an exciting exterior. Entrance to this unique home is gained through an air-lock-garden assuring privacy and comfort. Interior pleasures include a magnificent Great room and sunken conversation area with a fireplace. Sliding glass doors from the Great room open onto a large patio. Slightly elevated are the kitchen, dining, and breakfast rooms with bay windows. The master bedroom upstairs has a private deck.

First floor — 1,823 sq. ft.
Second floor — 488 sq. ft.
Basement — 530 sq. ft.
Garage — 797 sq. ft.

Total living area — 2,311 sq. ft.

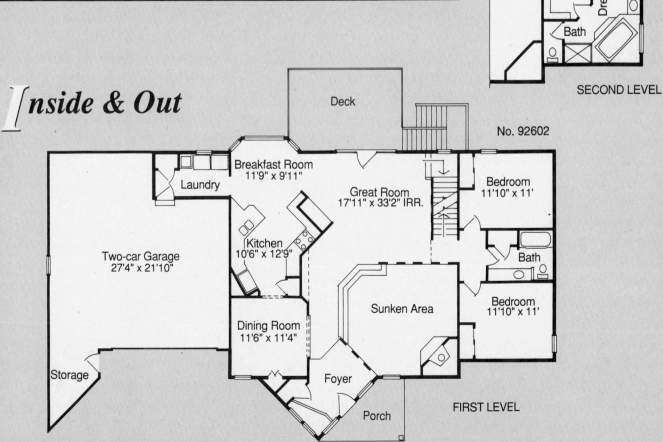

Master Bedroom
14'2" x 18'4"

Dressing

Bath

SECOND LEVEL

No. 92602

*I*nside & Out

Deck

Breakfast Room
11'9" x 9'11"

Laundry

Great Room
17'11" x 33'2" IRR.

Bedroom
11'10" x 11'

Kitchen
10'6" x 12'9"

Two-car Garage
27'4" x 21'10"

Bath

Dining Room
11'6" x 11'4"

Sunken Area

Bedroom
11'10" x 11'

Storage

Foyer

Porch

FIRST LEVEL

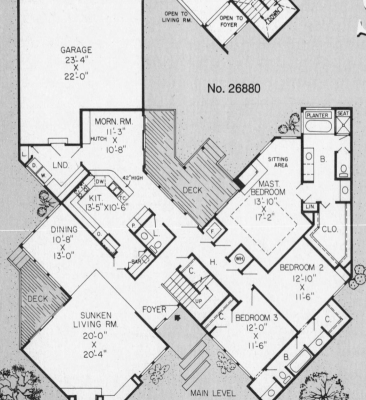

UPPER LEVEL

DECK

GAME ROOM
19'-0"
X
12'-0"

OPEN TO LIVING RM.

OPEN TO FOYER

DOWN

SKYLIGHT

No. 26880

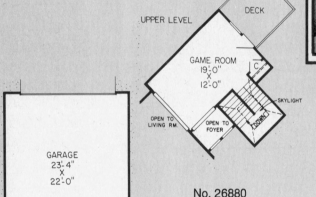

GARAGE
23'-4"
X
22'-0"

MORN. RM.
11'-3"
X
10'-8"
HUTCH

LND.

42" HIGH

KIT.
13'-5"X10'-6"

DINING
10'-8"
X
13'-0"

BAR

DECK

PLANTER SEAT

SITTING AREA

MAST. BEDROOM
13'-10"
X
17'-2"

B.

LIN

CLO.

H.

WH

C.

FOYER

UP

BEDROOM 3
12'-0"
X
11'-6"

C.

BEDROOM 2
12'-10"
X
11'-6"

C.

DECK

SUNKEN LIVING RM.
20'-0"
X
20'-4"

B

MAIN LEVEL

77'-0"

63'-6"

S'tep Down Into...

No. 26880

This all-wood dramatic home features a large living room that is one step down from the dining room and entryway. Two bedrooms share a bath, while the master bedroom shows a fireplace, sitting room and private bath. The large deck is accessible from both the master suite and the breakfast room. The upper level houses the game room with its own deck. Thick cedar shingles add interest to the roof, and the cedar siding requires little maintenance. This home would be an asset wherever it was built.

First floor — 2,357 sq. ft.
Second floor — 271 sq. ft.

Total living area — 2,628 sq. ft.

*L*uxurious
Living

*M*odern Beauty
Draws Much Attention

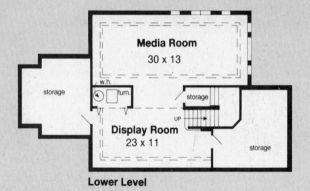

Media Room
30 x 13

storage

w.h.

furn.

storage

UP

Display Room
23 x 11

storage

Lower Level

This sunny, open plan says elegance everywhere you look. Each room has its own distinctive shape that's anything but commonplace. The island kitchen enjoys an unusual ceiling reveal and a window seat that looks out under the romantic trellis. The living and dining space, next to the kitchen, is united to allow for comfortable family time and has access to the backyard. A powder room, laundry and den complete the main floor. Upstairs, the masters of the house are spoiled by an oversized five-piece bath, a large walk-in closet and a private deck with a backyard view. Two more bedrooms, a bath, and a playroom are on this level. Downstairs, two massive rooms provide space for entertaining or relaxing with some friends.

Deck

No. 19257

slope   slope

MBr
13-4 x 13-4

slope

flat clg   skylights

shelf

open to living

railing

flat clg   DN

flat clg   slope

slope

shelf

Play room

slope

slope

open to foyer

lin.

flat clg

lin.

Br 2
11-8 x 12

Br 3
11-4 x 11

slope   slope

slope   slope

Second Floor

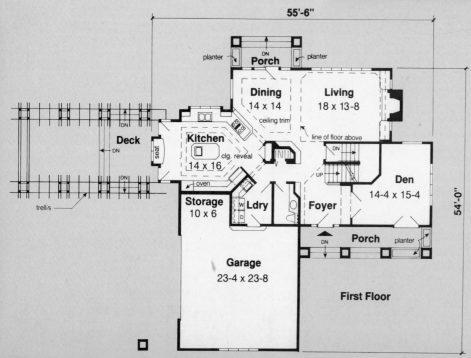

First floor — 1,296 sq. ft.
Second floor — 968 sq. ft.
Lower level — 1,296 sq. ft.
Garage — 656 sq. ft.

Total living area — 3,560 sq. ft.

55'-6"

54'-0"

planter

Porch

DN

planter

Dining
14 x 14

Living
18 x 13-8

ceiling trim

line of floor above

Kitchen

clg. reveal

14 x 16

oven

UP

DN

Den
14-4 x 15-4

Deck

DN

seat

DN

trellis

Storage
10 x 6

W
D

Ldry

Foyer

DN

Porch

planter

Garage
23-4 x 23-8

First Floor

Contemporary with Contrasts

No. 92600

This home is a study in contrasts in that it is a contemporary design based on forms and elements more often associated with New England communities. The foyer opens to both the dining room and Great room, which features a fireplace and a wetbar. In the kitchen one finds an angled work center. This area is convenient to the utility room and rear deck. The first floor master bedroom is secluded; it opens to a private deck and luxurious master bath that includes a large walk-in closet, separate tub, shower and double vanity. The two spacious bedrooms on the second floor share a divided bath with a double vanity. The loft has a spectacular view of both the foyer and Great room.

First floor — 2,245 sq. ft.
Second floor — 710 sq. ft.
Garage — 2-car

Total living area — 2,955 sq. ft.

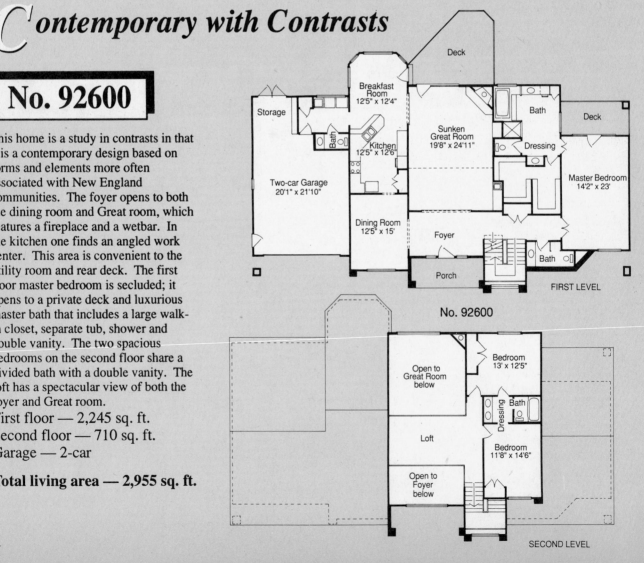

No. 92600

FIRST LEVEL

Deck
Breakfast Room 12'5" x 12'4"
Storage
Bath
Sunken Great Room 19'8" x 24'11"
Bath
Deck
Dressing
Kitchen 12'5" x 12'6"
Two-car Garage 20'1" x 21'10"
Master Bedroom 14'2" x 23'
Dining Room 12'5" x 15'
Foyer
Porch
Bath

SECOND LEVEL

Bedroom 13' x 12'5"
Open to Great Room below
Dressing
Bath
Loft
Bedroom 11'8" x 14'6"
Open to Foyer below

*S*unken Family Room Highlights Plan

No. 92601

The family room is a very special feature of this home. The room is open to the foyer, the breakfast area and the second floor balcony. Separating the family room from the breakfast area is a three-sided fireplace. The fireplace hearth forms the step into the sunken family room. The expansive second floor balcony looks out over the foyer into a half-circle window located in the sloped ceiling of the foyer. The master bedroom and master bath feature a sloped ceiling with a large, tall front window. Plant shelves hover over the bedroom's spacious walk-in closet. The kitchen counter also doubles as a serving bar and hutch for the adjoining dining room. The cabinets are accessible from both the dining room and kitchen.

First floor — 1,190 sq. ft.
Second floor — 890 sq. ft.
Garage — 2-car

Total living area — 2,080 sq. ft.

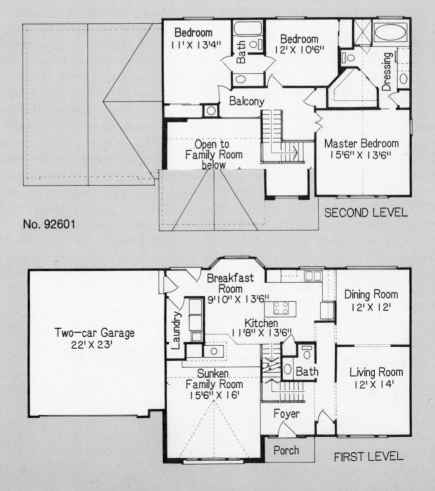

No. 92601

SECOND LEVEL

FIRST LEVEL

Enjoy the View

No. 20095

Step into the sunwashed foyer of this
contemporary beauty, and you'll be faced with a
choice. You can walk downstairs into a huge,
fireplaced rec room with built-in bar and
adjoining patio. Or, you can ascend the stairs to a
massive living room with sloping ceilings, a tiled
fireplace, and a commanding view of the
backyard. Sharing the view, the breakfast nook
with sunny bay opens to an outdoor deck. The
adjoining kitchen is just steps away from the
formal dining room, which features recessed
ceilings and overlooks the foyer. You'll also find
the master suite on this level, just past the powder
room off the living room. Three more bedrooms
and a full bath are located on the lower level.

Upper level — 1,448 sq. ft.
Lower level — 1,029 sq. ft.
Garage — 504 sq. ft.

Total living area — 2,477 sq. ft.

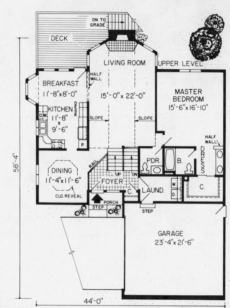

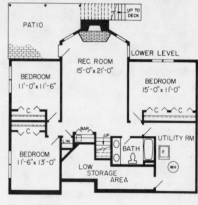

No. 20095

A Karl Kreeger Design

Courtyard Adds Interest

No. 22010

Well-defined contemporary lines are softened by
a semi-enclosed courtyard visible from the dining
area of this striking design. The 30-foot family
room is dominated by a fireplace, resulting in a
spacious but cozy area for entertaining. The
island kitchen merges with the dining nook. All
bedrooms are well-sized and the master bedroom
features it's own luxurious bath.

Main living area — 2,174 sq. ft.
Garage — 506 sq. ft.

Total living area — 2,174 sq. ft.

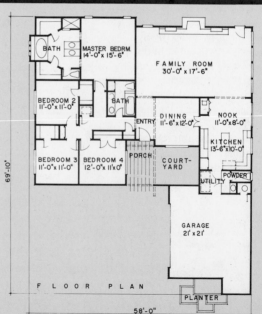

No. 22010

Sitting Room Shown in Unique Plan

No. 10292

With access to the sundeck, the sitting room in this two-story contemporary can function as a den, nursery or guest room. Abundantly supplied with cathedral ceilings and gable end windows, this airy design offers both a living room and a 23 ft. family room. A half-bath and laundry are located on the lower level. Closets are plentiful, and for entertaining, a formal dining room is provided.

First floor — 1,145 sq. ft.
Second floor — 864 sq. ft.
Basement — 1,145 sq. ft.
Garage — 568 sq. ft.

Total living area — 2,009 sq. ft.

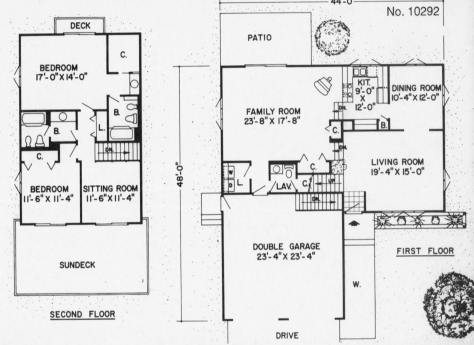

DECK

BEDROOM
17'-0" X 14'-0"

C.

B.

L.

B.

C.

BEDROOM
11'-6" X 11'-4"

SITTING ROOM
11'-6" X 11'-4"

DN.

SUNDECK

SECOND FLOOR

No. 10292

44'-0"

PATIO

KIT.
9'-0"
X
12'-0"

DINING ROOM
10'-4" X 12'-0"

FAMILY ROOM
23'-8" X 17'-8"

C.

B.

48'-0"

LIVING ROOM
19'-4" X 15'-0"

W
L

LAV.

C.

UP

DN.

DOUBLE GARAGE
23'-4" X 23'-4"

W.

FIRST FLOOR

DRIVE

Enchanting Entrance

No. 24300

A powerful entrance sets the tone for this affordable palace. The foyer, with its two-story ceiling and graceful turning staircase, is flanked by the living room and dining room — classic design that provides elegant sight lines. Beyond the foyer, this home is strikingly modern. The den/bedroom provides space to use in ways that suit your particular needs. Exceptional design shines in the unique arrangement of the family room, breakfast nook, kitchen, and laundry. This same design quality is apparent upstairs as well. The rooms are generous in size and arranged without wasting an inch of space. You'll appreciate the regal master suite each morning and night, especially the room-sized master bath with room for a relaxing whirlpool tub. Beauty, convenience, and practicality all combine to make this home a masterpiece.

First floor — 1,379 sq. ft.
Second floor — 858 sq. ft.
Basement — 1,383 sq. ft.
Garage — 454 sq. ft.

Total living area — 2,237 sq. ft.

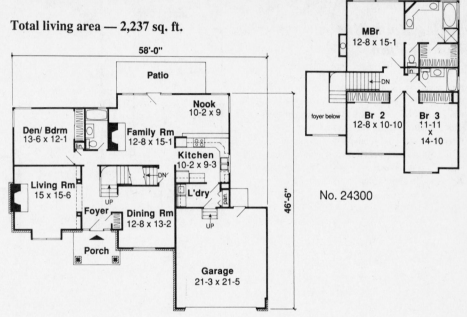

No. 24300

Stunning Split-Entry

No. 20143

This spacious split-entry home with a contemporary flavor is the perfect answer to the needs of your growing family. Imagine the convenience of a rec room with a built-in bar, powder room, and storage space on the garage level. Picture the luxury of your own, private master suite tucked off the foyer, featuring a walk-in closet, double-vanitied bath, and decorative ceilings. Active areas a few steps up include an expansive, fireplaced living room overlooking the foyer, an adjoining dining room graced with decorative ceilings and columns, and a skylit kitchen and breakfast room loaded with built-in amenities. Two bedrooms over the garage are steps away from the hall bath or the powder room.

Upper floor — 1,599 sq. ft.
Lower floor — 346 sq. ft.
Garage — 520 sq. ft.

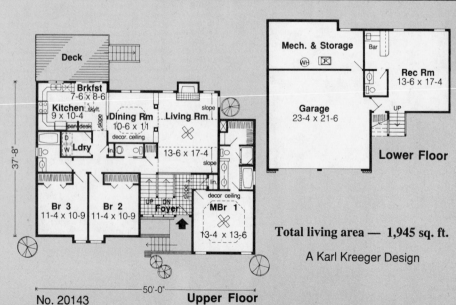

Total living area — 1,945 sq. ft.

A Karl Kreeger Design

No. 20143   **Upper Floor**

Best of Both Worlds

No. 20206

This dramatic home has the perfect blend of features. Traditional elegance outside encloses an up-to-date floor plan inside. Spacious living areas, perfect for entertaining, offset your private hideaway upstairs. The soaring, two-story foyer with a balcony above, graceful stairway, and huge living room with a see-thru fireplace, make this home a visual symphony. A unique staircase allows access from the bedrooms directly to the kitchen and hearth room, especially useful if the library is your home office. Upstairs, comfort and privacy are the rule — none of the bedrooms adjoin another, and each has its own walk-in closet and bath! You'll find the master suite, with its cozy sitting room and fireplace, is the perfect place to relax and get away from the world outside.

First floor — 2,032 sq. ft.
Second floor — 1,627 sq. ft.
Basement — 2,032 sq. ft.
Garage — 949 sq. ft.

Total living area — 3,659 sq. ft.

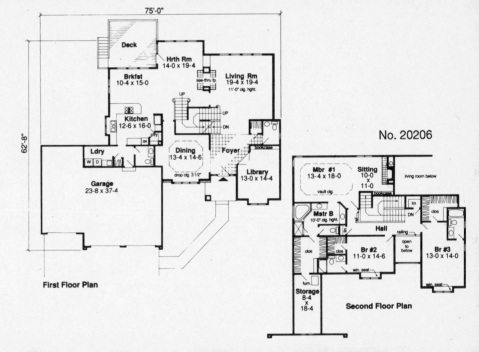

First Floor Plan

No. 20206

Second Floor Plan

Streetside Appeal

No. 20160

This three-bedroom beauty is loaded with convenience and charm. A traditional covered porch shelters entering guests. Lead them into the formal elegance of the living and dining room combination, divided by columns for a spacious feeling and a front-to-back view. When you want to kick off your shoes, show friends into the family room, where a two-way fireplace creates a warm, comfortable atmosphere. At the rear of the house, the kitchen and breakfast room adjoin in an open arrangement overlooking the rear deck. The master suite, tucked behind the garage in a quiet corner of the house, shares the backyard view. The open loft, that shares the second floor with two bedrooms and a full bath, would make a great rainy-day playroom for the kids.

First floor — 1,590 sq. ft.
Second floor — 567 sq. ft.
Basement — 1,576 sq. ft.
Garage — 456 sq. ft.

Total living area — 2,157 sq. ft.

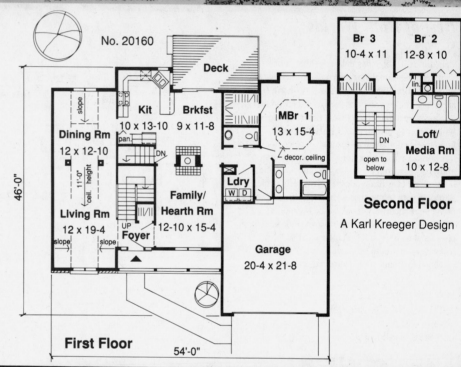

No. 20160

Deck

Kit 10 x 13-10

Brkfst 9 x 11-8

MBr 1 13 x 15-4
decor. ceiling

Dining Rm 12 x 12-10
pan.

11'-0" ceil. height

Living Rm 12 x 19-4
slope slope

UP **Foyer**

Family/ Hearth Rm 12-10 x 15-4

Ldry W D

Garage 20-4 x 21-8

46'-0"

First Floor 54'-0"

Br 3 10-4 x 11

Br 2 12-8 x 10

lin.

DN

Loft/ Media Rm 10 x 12-8

open to below

Second Floor

A Karl Kreeger Design

Outdoor-Lover's Dream

No. 20055

Here's a handsome home that presents a pretty face to passers-by, and provides lots of outdoor living space on a spacious rear deck. Soaring ceilings, oversized windows, and sliding glass doors unite the living room with the deck and rear yard. And, the handy kitchen makes meal service a breeze to either the dining room, adjoining breakfast bay, or deck. Tucked upstairs for quiet and privacy, three bedrooms open to a skylit hallway. The dramatic master suite features soaring ceilings and a private dressing area flanked by a full bath and walk-in closet.

First floor — 928 sq. ft.
Second floor — 773 sq. ft.
Basement — 910 sq. ft.
Garage — 484 sq. ft.

Total living area — 1,701 sq. ft.

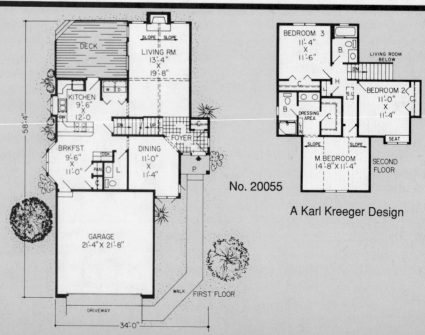

No. 20055

A Karl Kreeger Design

Cozy Contemporary Cape

No. 26744

The arched windows on the second floor give this great exterior a fun and cozy look and feel. The entryway is spacious and leads into the living room. The dining room and family room are conveniently located off the kitchen and breakfast area. The family room has a cozy fireplace for family gatherings. There is a powder room located off the kitchen. The master bedroom suite has a walk-in closet and a spacious separate bathroom. The second floor includes two additional bedrooms, a full bathroom and a full laundry room. This is a great floor plan for anyone.

First floor — 1,151 sq. ft.
Second floor — 893 sq. ft.
Basement — 1,047 sq. ft.
Garage — 493 sq. ft.

Total living area — 2,044 sq. ft.

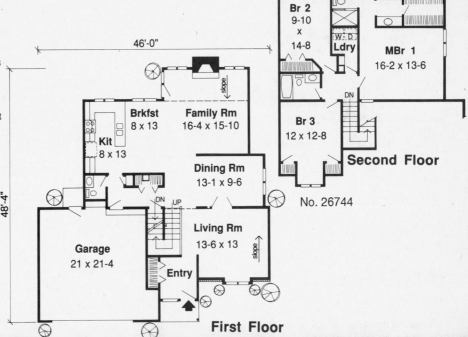

46'-0"

48'-4"

Brkfst 8 x 13
Kit 8 x 13
Family Rm 16-4 x 15-10
Dining Rm 13-1 x 9-6
DN UP
Garage 21 x 21-4
Living Rm 13-6 x 13
Entry

First Floor

Br 2 9-10 x 14-8
Ldry
MBr 1 16-2 x 13-6
W.D.
DN
Br 3 12 x 12-8

Second Floor

No. 26744

Compact Comfort

No. 10787

With its abundant windows and open plan, this sunny home will be warm and bright even on a chilly day. Soaring ceilings and a wall of stacked windows add dramatic volume to the spacious living room off the large central foyer. A step down, past the open railing, the dining room, so perfect for entertaining, completes the formal area of the house. For informal gatherings, walk into the kitchen/family room combination, separated by a handy breakfast bar. A cozy fireplace with wood storage and a built-in entertainment center combine with the efficient kitchen layout for a comfortable, convenient family area. Upstairs, you'll find three bedrooms and two full baths, including the luxury bath in the master suite.

First floor — 1,064 sq. ft.
Second floor — 708 sq. ft.
Basement — 1,064 sq. ft.
Garage — 576 sq. ft.

Total living area — 1,772 sq. ft.

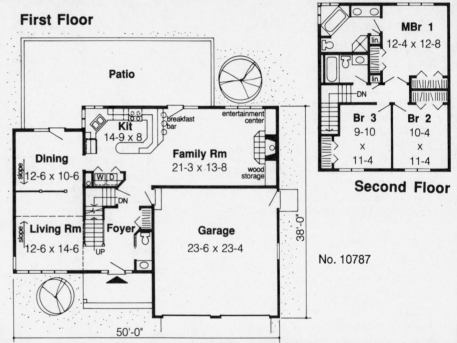

Classic Drama

No. 20165

The traditional clapboard exterior of this tidy home is deceiving. Step inside and you'll find drama on a grand scale. The central foyer, crowned by a balcony, slopes upward to meet the high ceilings of the fireplaced living room. At the rear of the house, you'll find a skylit dining room with a three-sided view of the adjoining deck. Just across the counter, the gourmet kitchen features a built-in desk and loads of cabinets. Three bedrooms share the second floor with two full baths. Rear bedrooms share the hall bath, but the master suite boasts a luxury bath complete with double vanities and a garden tub. Notice the generous closet and storage space throughout this exceptional, compact home.

First floor — 901 sq. ft.
Second floor — 864 sq. ft.
Basement — 901 sq. ft.
Garage — 594 sq. ft.

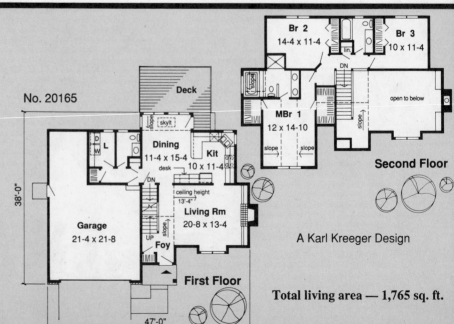

A Karl Kreeger Design

Total living area — 1,765 sq. ft.

Lofty Views

No. 20364

Thanks to vaulted ceilings and an absence of unnecessary walls, this compact gem feels larger than it really is. Step into the foyer and look up to a ceiling two stories high, an open staircase, and a spacious living and dining room arrangement with vaulted ceilings. At the core of the house, an efficient island kitchen opens to a sunny breakfast room with sliders to the rear patio. Whether you're serving a formal dinner, or a snack in the fireplaced family room, you're never more than a few steps away. Walk up the U-shaped stairs to a loft overlooking the scene below, which serves as a link to the three bedrooms and hall bath. The master suite features its own private bath with garden tub and double vanities.

First floor — 1,060 sq. ft.
Second floor — 990 sq. ft.
Basement — 1,060 sq. ft.
Garage — 462 sq. ft.

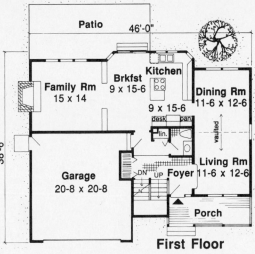

No. 20364

First Floor

Total living area — 2,050 sq. ft.

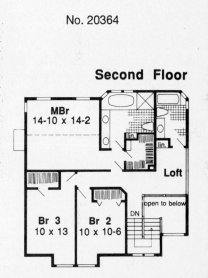

Second Floor

Passive Solar with Unique Great Room

No. 10380

Expanses of glass and rugged exposed beams
dominate the front of this design's six-sided
living center, creating a contemporary look that
would be outstanding in any setting. Angled
service and sleeping wings flow to the right and
left, creating unusually shaped rooms and spaces
for storage. Spiral stairs just inside the tiled entry
rise to a loft overlooking the Great room. All
rooms have sloped ceilings with R-38 insulation
while side walls call for R-24. Living and dining
possibilities are expanded by use of the rear patio
and deck. A full basement provides extra family
space to this plan.

First floor — 2,199 sq. ft.
Loft — 336 sq. ft.
Basement — 2,199 sq. ft.
Garage — 611 sq. ft.

Total living area — 2,535 sq. ft.

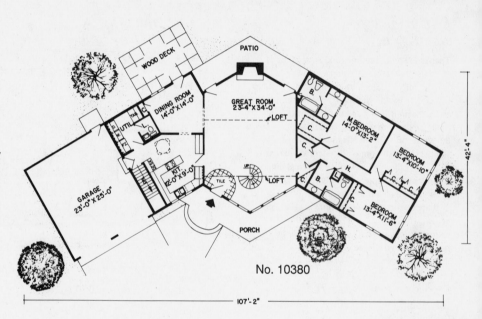

No. 10380

Dine on the Deck

No. 10679

Here's a sunshine special with a character all its
own. The covered porch opens to a spacious
foyer dominated by a U-shaped staircase. Step to
the right past the powder room, and you'll enter a
rear-facing master suite with his-n-her walk-in
closets and a luxurious bath overlooking the
deck. It's hard to miss the sunken living room to
the left, with its expansive stacked windows and
sloping ceiling pierced by skylights. A range-top
island separates the efficient kitchen from the
dining bay with windows on three side. The
window ledge over the sink is an ideal spot for an
indoor herb garden. Upstairs, you'll find a full
bath and two bedrooms, each with a walk-in
closet.

First floor — 1,945 sq. ft.
Second floor — 739 sq. ft.
Basement — 1,229 sq. ft.
Garage — 724 sq. ft.

Total living area — 2,684 sq. ft.

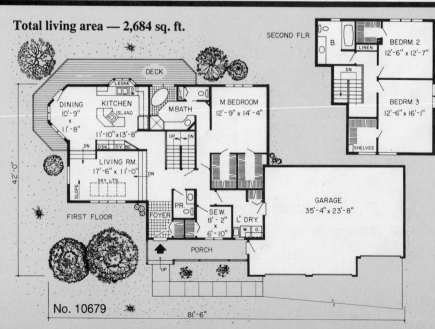

No. 10679

Dramatic Impressions

No. 20451

Picture yourself relaxing in the dappled sunlight of the partially covered deck that spans the rear of this unusual sprawling home. Entertaining will be easy in this spectacular setting, whether you choose the large, soaring living room off the vaulted skylit foyer or the cozy family room that shares the backyard view with the glass-walled breakfast room it adjoins. The kitchen easily serves every area, including the elegant formal dining room at the front of the house. Two bedrooms, tucked in a quiet spot off the family room, flank a full bath with double vanities. The master suite, tucked off behind the garage, features private deck access and a magnificent bath with a garden tub surrounded by glass block walls.

Main living area —2,084 sq. ft.
Basement —2,084 sq. ft.
Garage —2-car

Total living area — 2,084 sq. ft.

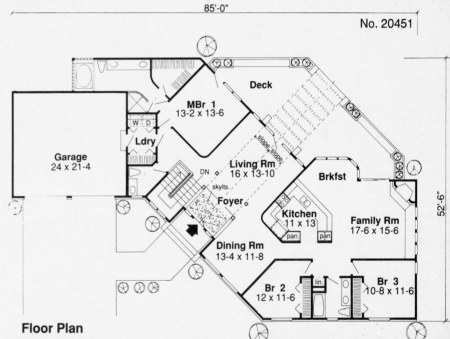

85'-0"

No. 20451

Deck

MBr 1
13-2 x 13-6

Garage
24 x 21-4

Ldry

W D

Living Rm
16 x 13-10

Brkfst

DN

skylts.

Foyer

Kitchen
11 x 13

pan. pan.

Family Rm
17-6 x 15-6

Dining Rm
13-4 x 11-8

Br 2
12 x 11-6

lin.

Br 3
10-8 x 11-6

52'-6"

Floor Plan

Master Suite Crowns Plan

No. 10394

The master bedroom suite occupies the entire second level of this passive solar design. The living room rises two stories in the front, as does the foyer, and can be opened to the master suite to aid in air circulation. Skylights in the sloping ceilings of the kitchen and master bath give abundant light to these areas. Angled walls, both inside and out, lend a unique appeal. An air-lock entry, 2x6 exterior studs, 6-inch concrete floor, and generous use of insulation help make this an energy efficient design.

First floor — 1,306 sq. ft.
Second floor — 472 sq. ft.
Garage — 576 sq. ft.

Total living area — 1,778 sq. ft.

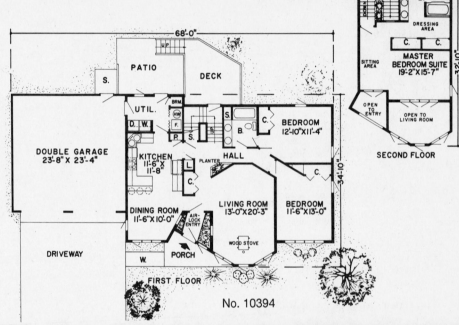

Deck Defies Gravity

No. 24306

This contemporary home is perfect for a mountainside with a far-reaching view. Imagine sitting by the fireplace in this large sunny living room and gazing into the distance. The spiral staircase adds a bit of style to this open plan. The galley kitchen has access to the rear deck and lies next to two bedrooms and a full bath with a convenient linen closet. The second floor has a loft, a roomy studio, a third bedroom with its own deck and a bathroom.

First floor — 841 sq. ft.
Second floor — 489 sq. ft.

Total living area — 1,330 sq. ft.

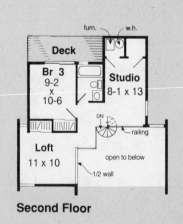

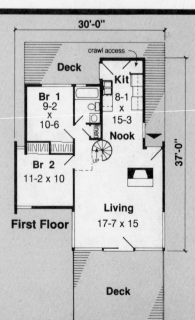

No. 24306

Master Suite on a Private Level

No. 26810

With its four floors staggered at half-level intervals, this house is both architecturally fascinating and effectively planned. Entering on the third level, one sees dining and sunken living rooms ahead on a space-expanded diagonal. The corridor kitchen extends into a traffic-free space open to living areas on one side. A deck makes the outdoors a natural part of all social areas. One half-level higher, the master bedroom connects to a study, a deck and a luxurious compartmental bathroom. On the second level, two smaller bedrooms have a landing with a bath and a convenient laundry. The lowest level of the house is a recreation basement. The framing of this house uses large studs and rafters spaced at wide intervals to cut construction time, reduce the need for lumber, and open deeper gaps for thicker insulating batts.

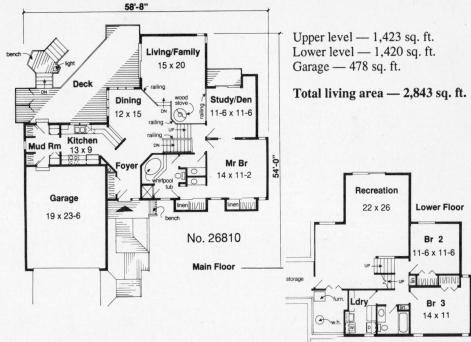

58'-8"

Deck

bench · light

DN

Living/Family
15 x 20

railing

Dining
12 x 15

wood stove

DN

railing

Study/Den
11-6 x 11-6

railing

UP

railing

DN

Kitchen
13 x 9

Mud Rm

Foyer

whirlpool tub

Mr Br
14 x 11-2

linen

linen

Garage
19 x 23-6

bench

No. 26810

54'-0"

Main Floor

Recreation
22 x 26

Lower Floor

storage

Br 2
11-6 x 11-6

UP

UP

furn.

Ldry

w.h.

W D

lin

Br 3
14 x 11

Upper level — 1,423 sq. ft.
Lower level — 1,420 sq. ft.
Garage — 478 sq. ft.

Total living area — 2,843 sq. ft.

Clapboard Contemporary

No. 20367

It's hard to miss the focal point of this magnificent contemporary home; the window wall that graces the dramatic two-story living room is a feast for the eyes, inside and out. And the open plan of this three-bedroom beauty adds even more excitement to its spacious ambience. Eat in the dining room that adjoins the living room, or have a snack by the fire in the sunken family room overlooking the rear deck. The nearby kitchen is convenient to both. Bedrooms share the second floor with two full baths. Be sure to notice the unique balcony room off the master suite.

First floor —1,108 sq. ft.
Second floor — 786 sq. ft.
Basement — 972 sq. ft.
Garage — 567 sq. ft.

Total living area — 1,894 sq. ft.

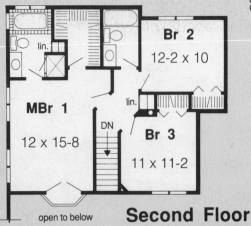

Second Floor

MBr 1
12 x 15-8

Br 2
12-2 x 10

Br 3
11 x 11-2

lin.

DN

open to below

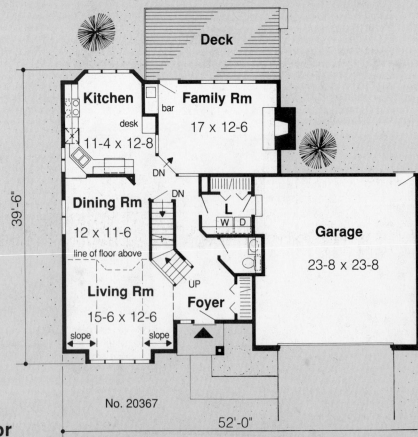

Deck

Kitchen
11-4 x 12-8
desk

Family Rm
17 x 12-6
bar

DN

Dining Rm
12 x 11-6

DN

L

W D

Garage
23-8 x 23-8

line of floor above

Living Rm
15-6 x 12-6

UP

Foyer

slope   slope

39'-6"

52'-0"

No. 20367

Attractive Rock Fireplace in Split Level

No. 10579

This split level design is built with superb architecture throughout which incorporates diagonal and vertical siding, a clerestory window and a beautiful bold rock fireplace. The lower level only houses a spacious two-car garage. The main floor has an expansive open-beamed, sloping ceiling and a fireplace adds gracious living features to this design. This plan comes equipped with an L-shaped kitchen with eating space. The foyer has closet space and the hallway comes with its own skylight that adds lots of natural lighting to this design. Three bedrooms are on the main floor. Two bedrooms have plenty of closet space and share one full bath. The master bedroom has a walk-in closet, a full bath area and a large square bay window area for more room.

Main level — 1,400 sq.ft
Loft — 142 sq. ft
Basement — 663 sq. ft.
Garage — 680 sq. ft.

Total living area — 1,542 sq. ft.

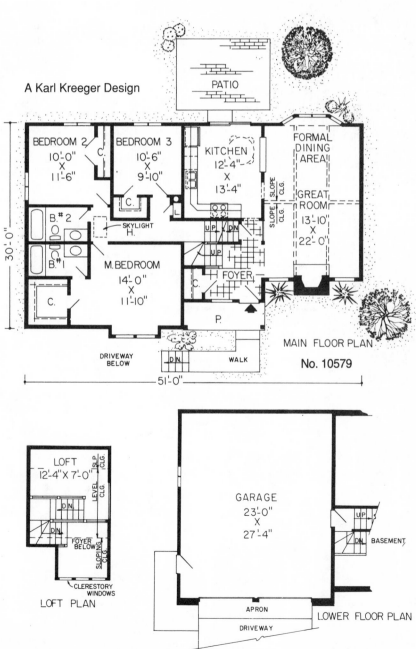

A Karl Kreeger Design

PATIO

BEDROOM 2
10'-0"
X
11'-6"

BEDROOM 3
10'-6"
X
9'-10"

KITCHEN
12'-4"
X
13'-4"

FORMAL DINING AREA

GREAT ROOM
13'-10"
X
22'-0"

SLOPE CLG.

SKYLIGHT H.

B. #2

B. #1

C.

M. BEDROOM
14'-0"
X
11'-10"

FOYER

C.

P.

30'-0"

DRIVEWAY BELOW

DN.

WALK

51'-0"

MAIN FLOOR PLAN

No. 10579

LOFT
12'-4" X 7'-0"

LEVEL CLG.

SLP CLG.

DN.

DN.

FOYER BELOW

SLOPING CLG.

CLERESTORY WINDOWS

LOFT PLAN

GARAGE
23'-0"
X
27'-4"

UP

DN. BASEMENT

APRON

LOWER FLOOR PLAN

DRIVEWAY

All This On One Level

No. 99619

A gracious feeling welcomes you inside the double entrance doors as you experience natural sky-lighting and flowing space enhanced by a high-sloped ceiling. Featured is the free-standing, heat-circulating fireplace surrounded by stone, to mantle height.

Sliding glass doors connect to a large rear terrace. The adjacent informal space of kitchen, dinette and family room share an openness. The dinette has access to a private dining terrace and the laundry room leading to the garage, basement or side service entrance. The private bedroom wing, accessed via the foyer, contains two large bedrooms, a bath and a master suite off a short corridor. This suite consists of a generously-sized bedroom connecting to a bath with double sinks and window.

Main living area — 1,629 sq. ft.
Lndry/mudroom — 107 sq. ft.
Garage — 424 sq. ft.
Basement — 1,457 sq. ft.

Total living area — 1,629 sq. ft.

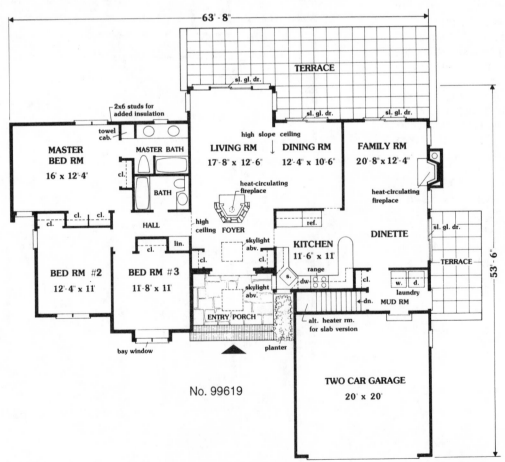

No. 99619

Triangular Entrance Extends Into Foyer

No. 99614

The gracious and spacious central foyer sets the tone for this luxurious 3 bedroom ranch home. The featured triangular ceiling of the entrance porch extends into the foyer. Recalling this triangular form are the bedroom bays. Other features include the large glazed bay the full width of the living room; the dinette which has a six-sided shape, four sides of which are glazed; three floor to ceiling glass panels are at the rear of the family room, one of which slides and gives access to the huge rear terrace; an angled kitchen counter acts as a snack bar convenient to the family room; high sloped-ceilings in the living and family rooms. In addition, the master bathroom is equipped with two basins, a shower stall, a whirlpool tub and a towel closet. The hall bathroom also has two basins and natural light.

Main living area — 2,282 sq. ft.
Lndry/mudroom — 114 sq. ft.
Garage — 509 sq. ft.
Basement — 2,136 sq. ft.

Total living area — 2,282 sq. ft.

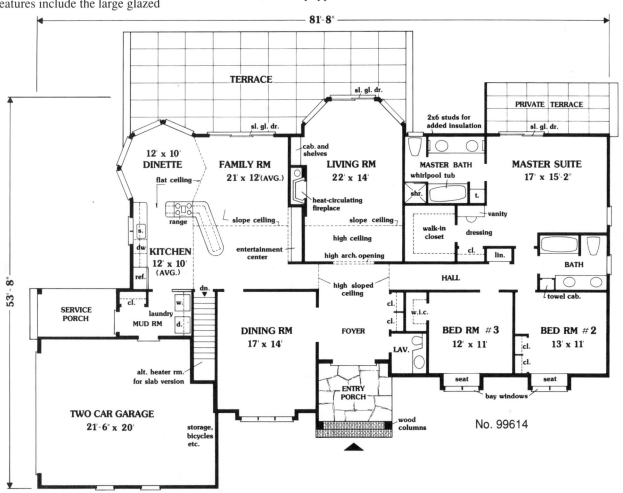

One-Level Budget Booster

No. 90937

Relax and enjoy the cost-saving advantages, and all the wonderful features, of this cozy ranch. From the central foyer, turn right to the sleeping wing. Tucked behind the garage away from active areas, the three bedrooms boast easy access to the utility room and two full baths. Or, walk straight past the general storage areas into the family eating nook and kitchen with sliders to the rear patio. Step down from the entry into the fireplaced, sunken living room. Bay windows and a wide-open view of the dining room give this formal area a delightful, sunny atmosphere.

Main living area — 1,238 sq. ft.
Garage — 399 sq. ft.
Width — 38 ft.
Depth — 52 ft.

Total living area — 1,238 sq. ft

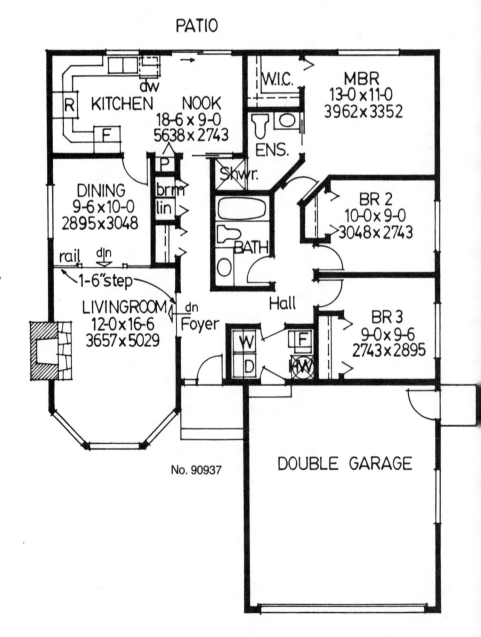

PATIO

KITCHEN
dw
R
F
NOOK
18-6 x 9-0
5638 x 2743

W.I.C.

MBR
13-0 x 11-0
3962 x 3352

ENS.

P
brm
lin

DINING
9-6 x 10-0
2895 x 3048

Shwr.

BR 2
10-0 x 9-0
3048 x 2743

BATH

rail   dn
1-6"step

LIVINGROOM
12-0 x 16-6
3657 x 5029

dn
Foyer

Hall

BR 3
9-0 x 9-6
2743 x 2895

W
D
F
KW

No. 90937

DOUBLE GARAGE

Family Living on One Level

No. 91027

Arches adorn exterior and interior spaces in this four-bedroom beauty. Look at the graceful openings between the sunken living and dining rooms just off the foyer and the massive half-round window and curved entryway facing the street. Walk past the den to family areas at the rear of the house, centering around the convenient island kitchen. An open plan keeps the cook from getting lonely while the kids are gathered around the fireplace or doing homework at the handy desk. And, the master suite is a special retreat. French doors unite the room with the backyard. At the end of a long day, the private spa is a plus you'll really appreciate.

Main living area — 2,174 sq. ft.

Total living area — 2,174 sq. ft.

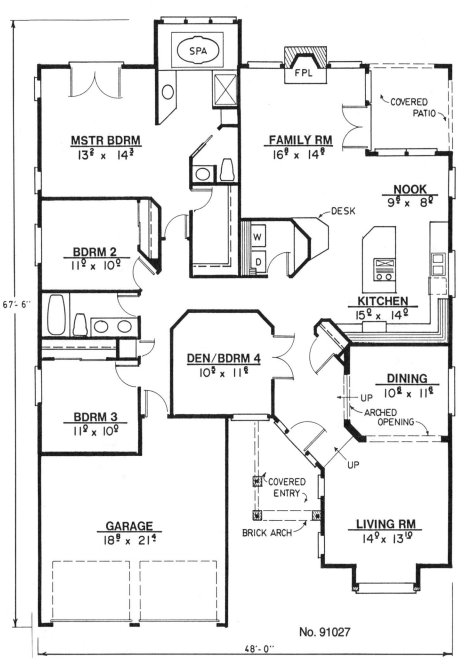

SPA

FPL

COVERED PATIO

MSTR BDRM
13² x 14³

FAMILY RM
16⁸ x 14⁸

NOOK
9⁸ x 8⁰

DESK

W
D

BDRM 2
11⁰ x 10⁰

KITCHEN
15⁰ x 14⁰

DEN/BDRM 4
10⁰ x 11⁸

DINING
10⁸ x 11⁸

UP

ARCHED OPENING

BDRM 3
11⁰ x 10⁰

UP

67'-6"

COVERED ENTRY

GARAGE
18⁸ x 21⁴

LIVING RM
14⁰ x 13¹⁰

BRICK ARCH

No. 91027

48'-0"

Tradition Combines With Contemporary

No. 99327

Traditional design elements such as half-round glass divider sash, covered front-entry porch, gable louvre detail, and wrap-around plant shelf under corner windows all help to create nostalgic appeal. A dramatic view awaits guests at the entry with a vaulted ceiling above the living room with clerestory glass, fireplace corner windows with half-round transom, and a long view through the dining room sliders to the rear deck. The main floor master suite has corner windows, walk-in closet and private bath access.

First floor — 858 sq. ft.
Second floor — 431 sq. ft.
Basement — 858 sq. ft.
Garage — 2-car

Total living area — 1,289 sq. ft.

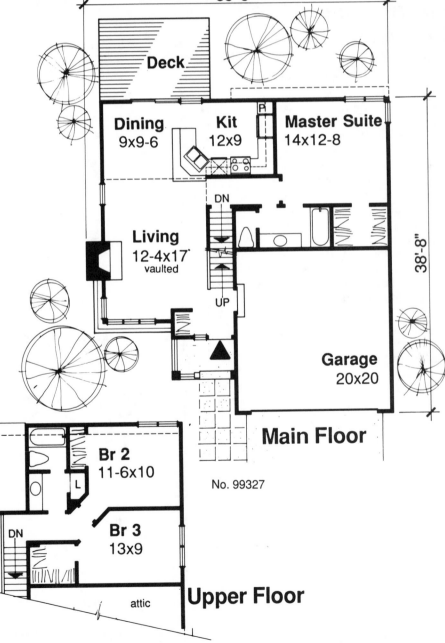

38'-8"

Deck

Dining
9x9-6

Kit
12x9

Master Suite
14x12-8

DN

Living
12-4x17'
vaulted

UP

38'-8"

Garage
20x20

Main Floor

No. 99327

Br 2
11-6x10

open to below

DN

Br 3
13x9

attic

Upper Floor

Abundant Windows Add Outdoor Feeling

No. 99310

Now here's a three-bedroom house your family will want to call home. From its traditional front porch to the breakfast bay overlooking the patio, this country charmer has an inviting appeal that's hard to resist. With conveniences like a built-in bar in the dining room, an efficient kitchen with a range-top island, built-in planning desk and pantry, and two-and-a-half baths to accommodate your busy family, you won't want to resist! Add the excitement of a vaulted, fireplaced living room with windows on three sides, an open staircase flooded with natural light, and a dramatic master suite with private, double-vanitied bath, and you've got the perfect place to raise your family.

First floor — 1,160 sq. ft.
Second floor — 797 sq. ft.
Garage — 2-car

Total living area — 1,957 sq. ft.

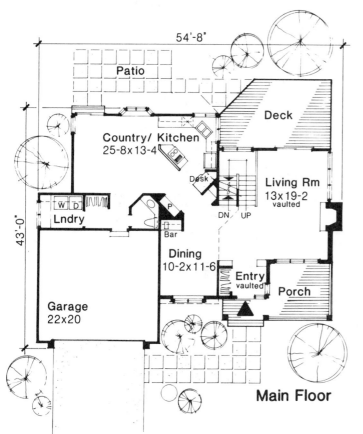

Main Floor

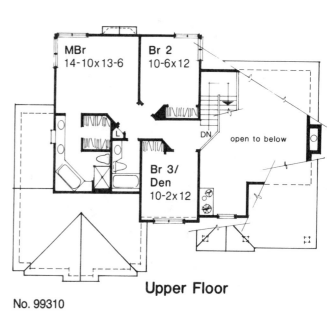

No. 99310

Upper Floor

Good Use of Space

No. 91707

With only the two bedrooms and a bathroom upstairs, this medium sized home is equally well adapted to a family with older children, or empty nesters who wish to have space to accomodate grandchildren, and to entertain without feeling cramped. The entryway and formal living room are vaulted to the second floor giving a feeling of vastness to visitors and family alike. In fact, the landing at the top of the curving stairway, overlooks the living room. The kitchen, with both a garden window and a bay window, is spacious and bright. This design makes excellent use of oddly shaped spaces. A hutch is tucked into an angle in the dining room, a fireplace in another in the family room, and a small angled half bath is conveniently close to everything. The master suite has an oversized tub and a shower, both brightened by a skylight and glass blocks. The two-car garage includes extra space for a workbench and/or storage space.

First floor — 1,940 sq. ft.
Second floor — 552 sq. ft.
Garage — 608 sq. ft.

Total living area — 2,492 sq. ft.

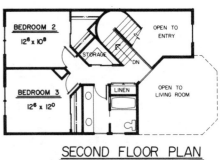

SECOND FLOOR PLAN

No. 91707

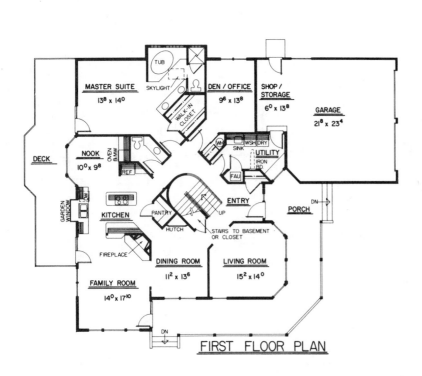

FIRST FLOOR PLAN

Contemporary Classic with a Custom Look

No. 99314

A curving staircase lit from above, crowns the entry of this beautiful wood and fieldstone contemporary. To the right, a well-apppointed kitchen features an angular nook just perfect for your breakfast table. The Great room straight ahead soars two stories, for an outdoor feeling accentuated by a massive fireplace and sliders to the rear deck. Corner windows make the dining area a pleasant spot to enjoy a dinner with friends. To the left, past the powder room, the master suite features a bump-out window seat, and a private bath with double vanities. An open loft overlooking the Great room shares the second floor with a second bedroom and another full bath.

First floor — 1,044 sq. ft.
Second floor — 454 sq. ft.
Garage — 2-car

Total living area — 1,498 sq. ft.

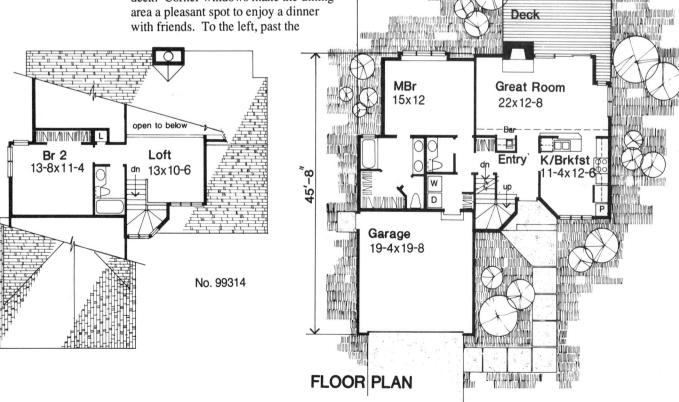

No. 99314

FLOOR PLAN

A Warm Welcome

No. 92013

This exciting two-story home has a large roof mass with multiple gables and wrap-around porch. The two-story entry offers views to outside living spaces through both the living room and breakfast area. The first floor den offers the flexibility of a home office or guest bedroom. The large island kitchen and breakfast area are open to a family room with access to the three-season sun room and rear deck. Formal dining room with trayed ceiling and formal living room round out the main floor. Upstairs features include 2 bedrooms, bath, laundry facilities, and a balcony overlooking the entry below.

First floor — 1,336 sq. ft.
Second floor — 1,015 sq. ft.
Basement — 1,336 sq. ft.
Garage — 496 sq. ft.

Total living area — 1,749 sq. ft.

MAIN FLOOR

No. 92013

UPPER FLOOR

One-Level Living with a Wide-Open Feeling

No. 99313

An arched transom window high over the entry makes a dramatic impression on guests entering this brick and stucco beauty. And, the excitement continues as you show them into the vaulted, fireplaced Great room with its full wall view of the adjoining deck and backyard beyond sliding glass doors. Serve dinner away from the bustle of the efficient kitchen, or in the greenhouse atmosphere of the informal breakfast nook. And, when the guests go home, walk past the den to your master suite retreat, which features access to a private corner of the deck, both walk-in shower and tub, and double vanities. The front bedroom adjoins a full, two-part bath.

Main living area — 1,955 sq. ft.
Garage — 3-car

Total living area — 1,955 sq. ft.

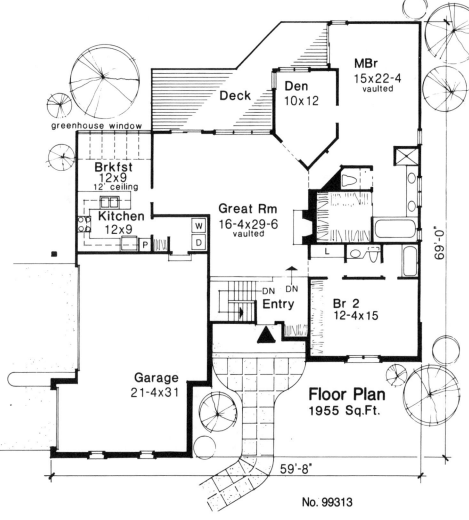

Deck

greenhouse window

Den
10x12

MBr
15x22-4
vaulted

Brkfst
12x9
12' ceiling

Kitchen
12x9

Great Rm
16-4x29-6
vaulted

W
D
P
L

Br 2
12-4x15

DN   DN
Entry

69'-0"

Garage
21-4x31

Floor Plan
1955 Sq.Ft.

59'-8"

No. 99313

Master Suite Is Home Away From Home

No. 91706

Inside this plan, find bright quarry tile floors in the entryway, kitchen, family room and utility room. Outside, a tile roof shelters its owners for many years to come. Plants will flourish in the bright kitchen/family room, doubled in size by an attached pre-fabricated solarium. The entryway and living room are vaulted to the second floor and bathed in light by wide bay windows. With the simple addition of a door to the right, off the front entry deck, the bright, vaulted-den could easily become a home office. The master bedroom is secluded on the second floor, away from two identical bedrooms on the first floor. Skylights bring natural light into the spa and water closet, and the huge walk-in closet provides ample room for storage as well as clothing.

First floor — 1,856 sq. ft.
Second floor — 618 sq. ft.
Garage — 704 sq. ft.

Total living area — 2,474 sq. ft.

No. 91706

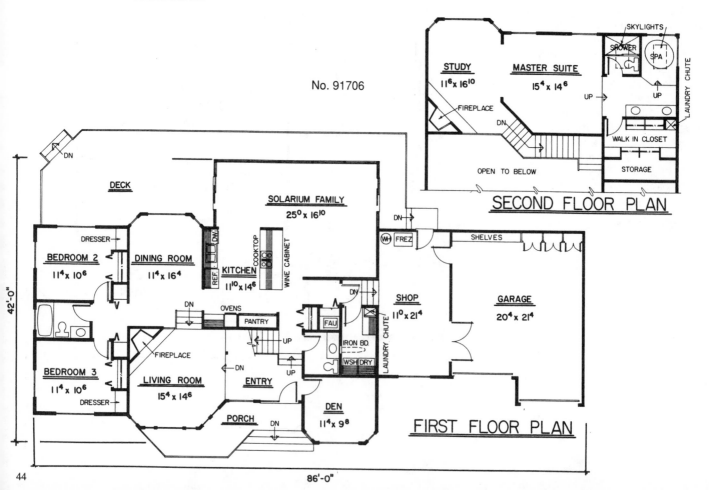

Warm, Inviting, and Contemporary

No. 91403

Two fireplaces and a wealth of oversized windows give this home an airy yet cozy atmosphere you'll enjoy for years. A graceful, curving balcony softens the two-story foyer, and leads to three bedrooms and two full baths upstairs. You'll love the master suite, with its own private deck, and double-vanitied bath with both tub and walk-in shower. To the left of the foyer, the family room, breakfast nook, and kitchen with a range-top island unite in a spacious, open arrangement just perfect for informal living. When you want to entertain in style, choose the elegant dining room, accessible to a huge rear deck through French doors.

The adjacent living room features a built-in entertainment center. Specify a crawlspace or basement when ordering this plan.

First floor — 1,459 sq. ft.
Second floor — 1,025 sq. ft.
Garage — 672 sq. ft.

Total living area — 2,484 sq. ft.

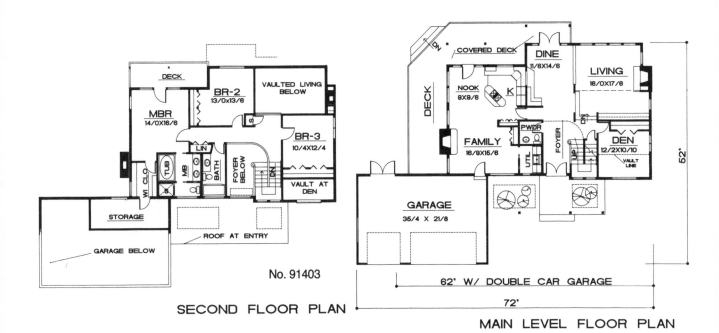

No. 91403

SECOND FLOOR PLAN

MAIN LEVEL FLOOR PLAN

A Lifetime Home

No. 91662

This beautiful, very popular plan has been re-designed to allow accessibility for a lifetime of use. It has built-in features that make modification possible to accommodate the permanently disabled, the elderly or even temporary disabled due to sports injuries, surgery, etc... Wider hallways and doors, specially designed baths and kitchen, and low profile thresholds are among some of the features you will find.

Main floor — 2,167 sq. ft.
Lower Floor — 1,154 sq. ft.

Total living area — 3,321 sq. ft.

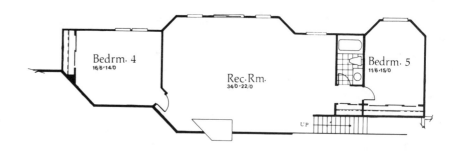

No. 91662

Bedrm. 4
16,6·14,0

Rec·Rm.
34,0·22,0

Bedrm. 5
11,6·15,0

UP

LOWER FLOOR

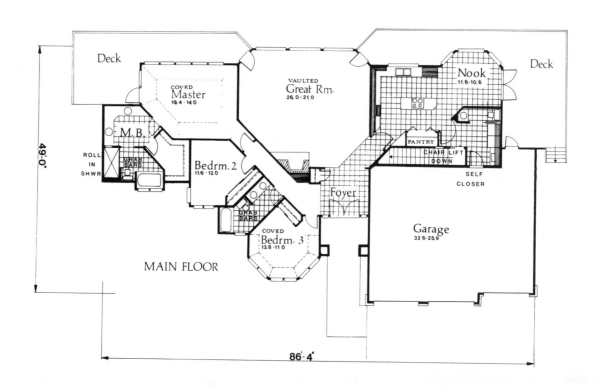

Deck

COV'RD
Master
19,4·14,0

Deck

VAULTED
Great Rm.
26,0·21,0

Nook
11,6·10,6

M.B.

ROLL
IN
SHWR

GRAB
BARS

Bedrm. 2
11,6·12,0

PANTRY

CHAIR LIFT
DOWN

SELF
CLOSER

GRAB
BARS

Foyer

Garage
32,6·25,9

COV'RD
Bedrm. 3
13,8·11,0

49'-0"

MAIN FLOOR

86'-4'

At Home on a Hillside

No. 90559

Here's a multi-level beauty designed for the family that enjoys entertaining. Show guests into the beautiful living room that shares the entry level with the private master suite. Dine in formal elegance overlooking the living room fireplace. The kitchen and a handy powder room are just a few steps away. Or, for a casual evening, the comfortable family room, with its built-in bar and proximity to the kitchen and patio, is an excellent choice. When bedtime approaches, you're assured of a quiet atmosphere with three bedrooms and a full bath tucked a half-flight up, away from active areas.

First floor — 2,388 sq. ft.
Second floor — 709 sq. ft.
Garage — 3-car

Total living area — 3,097 sq. ft.

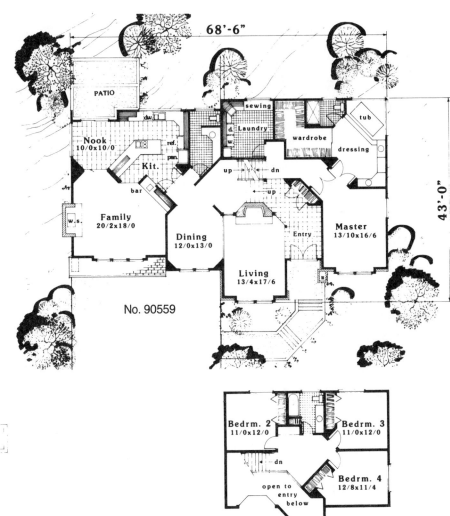

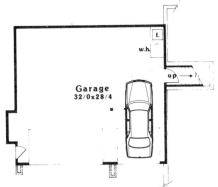

Sunny and Open

No. 91660

The impressive facade of this beautiful home hints at the sunny, open atmosphere inside. The foyer is inviting with its vaulted ceiling, flanked by a private study and formal living room. The kitchen is spacious with an island in the center that accommodates an eating area as well as a work surface. A separate nook area which is open to above, has many windows. This complements the wonderful family room which flows nicely off the kitchen area. The kitchen has a unique curved wall with beautiful French doors and many windows. The upper level is spacious and efficiently layed out with master bed/bath and three bedrooms with a bonus room over the three-car garage.

First floor — 1,843 sq. ft.
Second floor — 1,371 sq. ft.
Bonus room — 221 sq. ft.
Garage — 3-car

Total living area — 3,435 sq. ft.

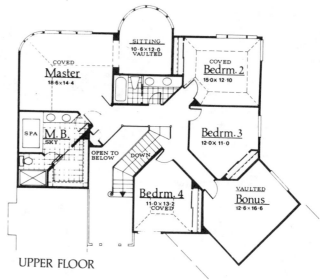

UPPER FLOOR

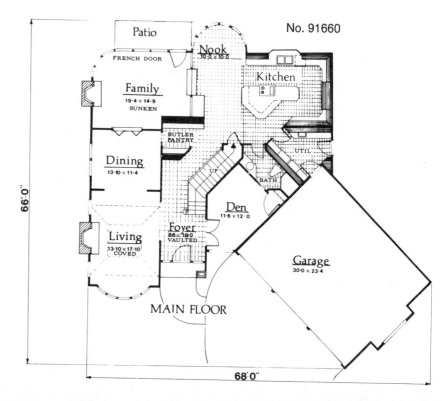

No. 91660

MAIN FLOOR

Spacious Kitchen Completes Special Design

No. 91654

This home has it all... beauty, luxury and livability. Marvel at the coved ceilings, large picture windows, and graciously curved staircase. Enjoy the luxury and unwind in front of the fireplace in the family or living room, or languish in the spa in the spacious master suite. This home also boasts a large U-shaped kitchen centered around a complete cooking island; a formal dining room for family and friends; three bathrooms; a bonus room; and optional upper floor.

Main floor — 1,233 sq. ft.
Upper floor — 902 sq. ft.
Bonus room — 168 sq. ft.

Total living area — 2,135 sq. ft.

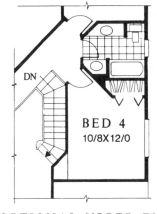

No. 91654

OPTIONAL UPPER FLOOR

BED 4
10/8 X 12/0

DN

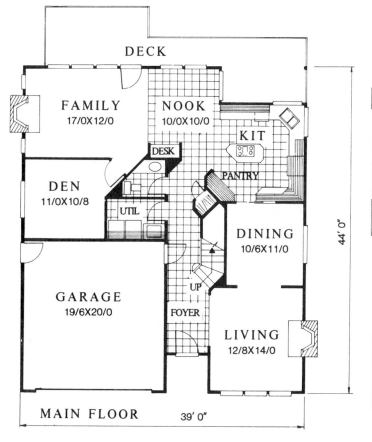

DECK

FAMILY
17/0 X 12/0

NOOK
10/0 X 10/0

KIT

DESK

PANTRY

DEN
11/0 X 10/8

UTIL

DINING
10/6 X 11/0

UP

FOYER

GARAGE
19/6 X 20/0

LIVING
12/8 X 14/0

44' 0"

MAIN FLOOR   39' 0"

MASTER
15/0 X 12/0

SPA

MB

BED 2
11/0 X 10/0

BED 3
11/0 X 10/8

WIC

DN

OPEN
TO
BELOW

BONUS
12/0 X 14/0

UPPER FLOOR

Pretty Palladium

No. 91627

This easy-care home combines classic elements with modern zoning for carefree living on a grand scale. The octagonal great hall directs traffic flow throughout the house: to the front-facing den, to the elegant coved living room with its triple arched windows and cozy fireplace, to the informal areas at the rear of the house, and the bedroom wing tucked behind the garage. You'll love the gourmet kitchen, with its range-top island, that overlooks the bay dining nook and coved, fireplaced family room. And, the adjoining rear deck is a nice spot for a warm-weather party. Three bedrooms include an exquisite master suite that features a private, double-vanitied bath with a garden spa, a walk-in closet, and a bay window view of the backyard.

Main living area — 2,097 sq. ft.
Garage — 2-car

Total living area — 2,097 sq. ft.

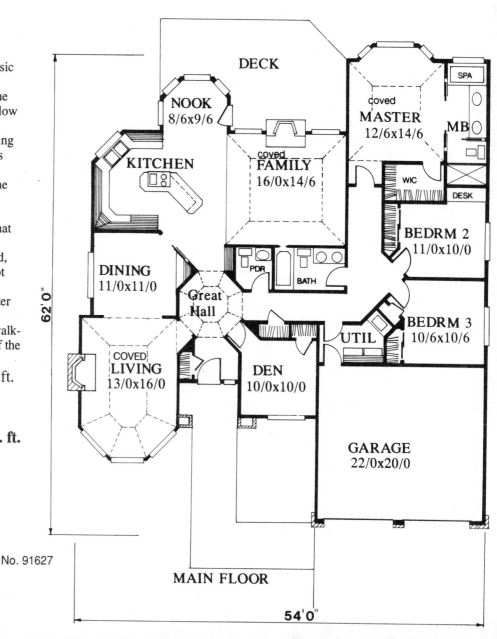

No. 91627

MAIN FLOOR

54' 0"

Convertible Castle

No. 91617

Bay windows provide three-way views throughout this gabled beauty, making it an ideal home for an attractive setting. Wherever you build this magnificent brick and stucco classic, you'll love the sunny atmosphere in every room, the intelligent separation of active and quiet areas, and the first-floor master suite with private bath. The central foyer separates the den from the elegant, coved living and dining room arrangement. Step back to the fireplaced family room, situated next to the island kitchen so the cook can enjoy the crackling fire and family companionship. The second floor offers endless possiblities suited to your lifestyle. And, the centrally-located bath with double vanities will be an asset on busy mornings.

First floor — 1,622 sq. ft.
Second floor — 529 sq. ft.
Bonus room — 269 sq. ft.
Garage — 2-car

Total living area — 2,151 sq. ft.

No. 91617

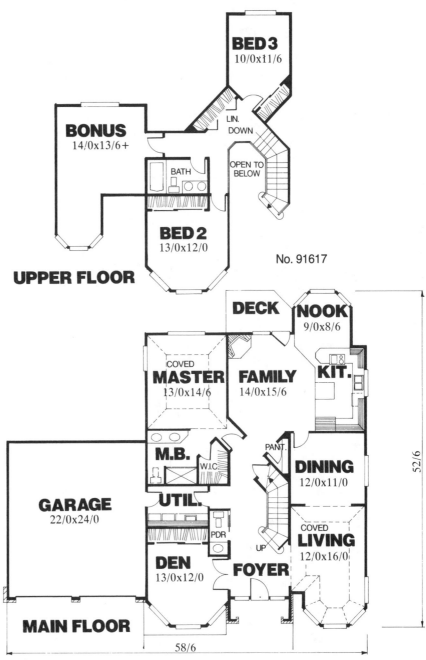

UPPER FLOOR

BED 3
10/0x11/6

BONUS
14/0x13/6+

BATH

LIN. DOWN

OPEN TO BELOW

BED 2
13/0x12/0

DECK

NOOK
9/0x8/6

MASTER
13/0x14/6 (COVED)

FAMILY
14/0x15/6

KIT.

M.B.

W.I.C

PANT.

DINING
12/0x11/0

GARAGE
22/0x24/0

UTIL.

PDR

UP

COVED
LIVING
12/0x16/0

DEN
13/0x12/0

FOYER

MAIN FLOOR

52/6

58/6

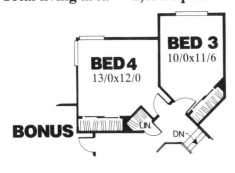

BED 4
13/0x12/0

BED 3
10/0x11/6

BONUS

LIN.

DN

Main Floor Study
Sure to be a Hit

No. 90968

Study this plan very carefully, it has many features in a relatively small area. The main floor study with a view and access to the front entry presents many possibilities...it would make a great home office. The bonus room on the second floor could be used as a fourth bedroom or playroom, and just look at the amenities offered in the master suite.

First floor — 1,268 sq. ft.
Second floor — 912 sq. ft.
Bonus room — 224 sq. ft.
Basement — 1,200 sq. ft.
Garage — 421 sq. ft.
Width — 41'-0"
Depth — 52'-0"

Total living area — 2,404 sq. ft.

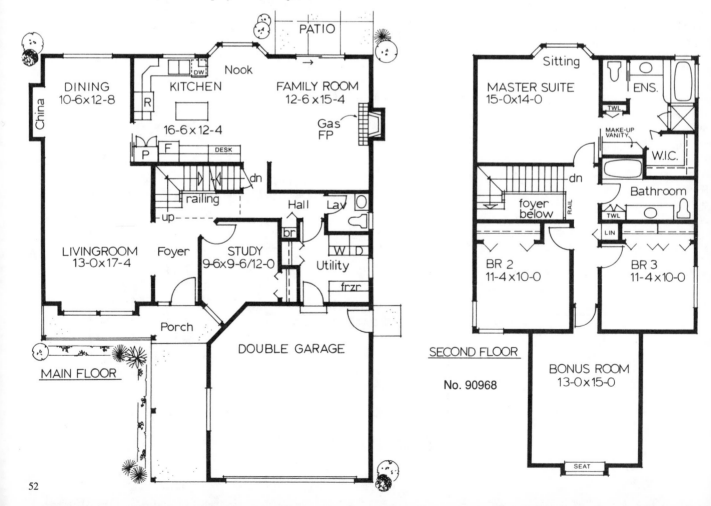

Two-Story Arched Window Makes Dramatic Statement

No. 91412

Old and new unite in this attractive, three-bedroom home with a rear view orientation. A gabled roof, large covered porch, and bump-out windows add traditional appeal to the open plan. The spacious family room-kitchen combination, which shares a fireplace with the sunken living room, will give you a chance to keep tabs on the kids as you prepare supper. And, the proximity of the kitchen to the impressive, vaulted dining room at the front of the house will make entertaining a breeze. There's a roomy feeling upstairs, too, with a sunny balcony overlooking the dining room and entry. Notice the private deck, the double-vanitied bath, and huge walk-in closet in the master suite. Specify a crawlspace or basement when ordering this plan.

First floor — 1,416 sq. ft.
Second floor — 1,056 sq. ft.
Garage — 504 sq. ft. or 729 sq. ft.

Total living area — 2,472 sq. ft.

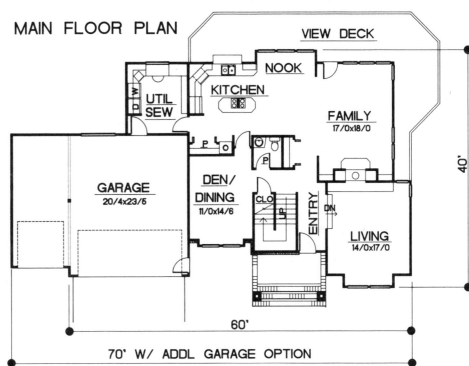

MAIN FLOOR PLAN

VIEW DECK

NOOK

KITCHEN

UTIL SEW

FAMILY
17/0x18/0

GARAGE
20/4x23/5

DEN/
DINING
11/0x14/6

CLO

ENTRY

LIVING
14/0x17/0

40'

60'

70' W/ ADDL GARAGE OPTION

No. 91412

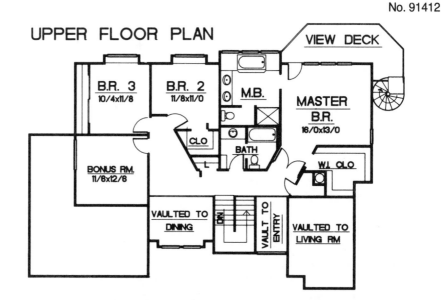

UPPER FLOOR PLAN

VIEW DECK

B.R. 3
10/4x11/8

B.R. 2
11/8x11/0

M.B.

MASTER
B.R.
18/0x13/0

CLO

BATH

W.I. CLO

BONUS RM.
11/8x12/6

VAULTED TO
DINING

DN

VAULT TO
ENTRY

VAULTED TO
LIVING RM

Streetside View

No. 91620

The floor-to-ceiling windows in the living room and den of this handsome home hint at the outdoor feeling you'll find inside. The foyer leads into the kitchen, centrally located at the heart of the home. To the left, the vaulted living room adjoins the sunny dining room in a flowing, spacious arrangement. To the right, past the den, you'll find a full bath, bedroom, and vaulted master suite with a private, double-vanitied bath and walk-in closet. The vaulted family room, crowned by a cozy fireplace, unites with the kitchen, glass-walled nook, and covered porch in one, expansive space your family will enjoy for years.

Main living area—1,633 sq. ft.
Garage — 2-car

Total living area — 1,633 sq. ft.

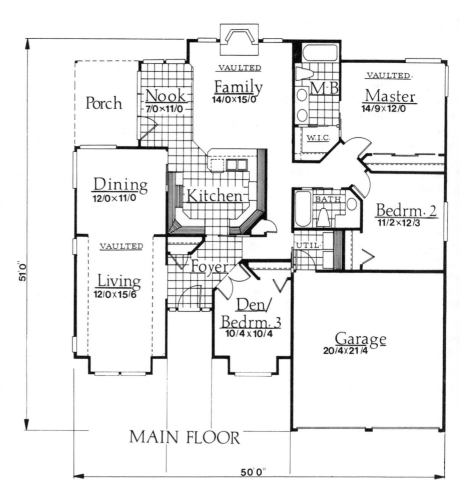

Porch

Nook
7/0×11/0

VAULTED
Family
14/0×15/0

M·B

VAULTED
Master
14/9×12/0

W.I.C.

Dining
12/0×11/0

Kitchen

BATH

Bedrm. 2
11/2×12/3

VAULTED

Living
12/0×15/6

Foyer

UTIL.

Den/
Bedrm. 3
10/4×10/4

Garage
20/4×21/4

51'0"

MAIN FLOOR

50'0"

No. 91620

54

Bright and Beautiful

No. 91008

Imagine the attention the brightly-lit stair tower of this smart contemporary will attract after dark. From the bay-windowed kitchen and bedroom to the fireplaced living room, the angles of the tower are mirrored in the shapes of every room. Watch your guests arrive from the convenient kitchen at the front of the house or the balcony upstairs. You'll enjoy the privacy of entertaining in the formal dining room at the rear of the house, or the covered patio just outside. At day's end, the master suite is a roomy and welcoming retreat.

First floor — 1,153 sq. ft.
Second floor — 493 sq. ft.

Total living area — 1,646 sq. ft.

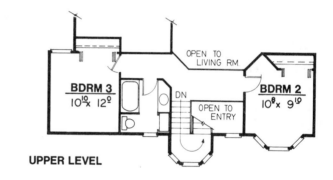

UPPER LEVEL

BDRM 3
10¹⁰ x 12⁰

OPEN TO LIVING RM

DN

OPEN TO ENTRY

BDRM 2
10⁸ x 9¹⁰

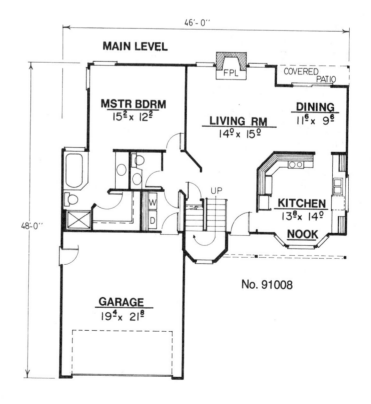

MAIN LEVEL

46'-0"

48'-0"

MSTR BDRM
15² x 12²

LIVING RM
14⁰ x 15⁰

FPL

COVERED PATIO

DINING
11⁸ x 9⁶

UP

KITCHEN
13⁸ x 14⁰

NOOK

W
D

GARAGE
19⁴ x 21⁸

No. 91008

Carefree and Cozy

No. 91618

The multiple peaks of this one-level home hint at the intriguing plan you'll find inside. The central foyer opens to a many-sided great hall, which offers access to every area of the house. To the left, the fireplaced living room with coved ceilings and massive front window flows into a formal dining room with built-in corner cabinet. Step back to the island kitchen that adjoins a sunny breakfast bay and comfortable family room overlooking the deck. You'll find three bedrooms tucked behind the garage, off a hallway that leads past the den, powder room, full bath, and utility room with garage access. The master suite at the rear of the house is a special treat, with its bay window, coved ceilings, and private bath with double vanities and garden spa.

Main living area — 2,087 sq. ft.
Garage — 2-car

Total living area — 2,087 sq. ft.

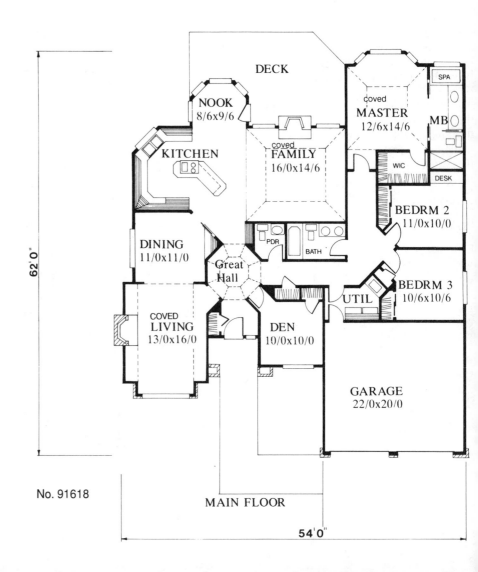

No. 91618

MAIN FLOOR

Simple Elegance

No. 90578

Clever use of efficient traffic flow and generous ceiling heights bring immediate excitement to this floor plan. With transom windows adding light to the eleven-and-a-half foot ceilings in the dining, living, and den area, this simply structured home contains many features found beyond the 2,355 square feet within. Efficient, yet adequate hallspace allows more space to be devoted to the living spaces around the house. An arched transom over the entry door invites you in for closer inspection as well as providing ample light for the raised entry platform which gives a commanding view of the formal living areas as well as the entrance to the family and sleeping areas. A modern island kitchen highlights the family area complete with a bayed breakfast nook. Be sure to notice how, in addition to enhancing the curb appeal to the home, the angled garage also allows this house to adapt to cul-de-sac lots or uneven lot lines.

First floor — 1,455 sq. ft.

Second floor — 900 sq. ft.

Garage — 620 sq. ft.

Total living area — 2,355 sq. ft.

No. 90578

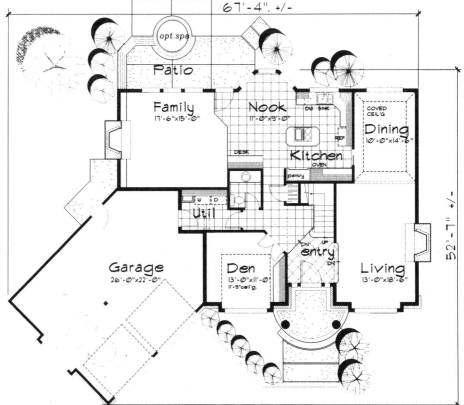

Columns Adorn Entry

No. 91427

This comtemporary home with traditional overtones features a centrally located staircase that is open to the vaulted living room which is complete with fireplace and built-in bar. The secluded master bedroom suite boasts a custom bath, walk-in closet and a spiral staircase to the sunspace below which is also open to the family room. The first floor bedrooms share a full bath.

First floor — 1,248 sq. ft.
Second floor — 723 sq. ft.
Sunspace — 116 sq. ft.

Total living area — 1,971 sq. ft.

No. 91427

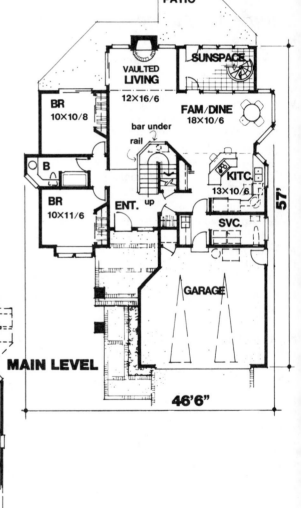

MAIN LEVEL

46'6"

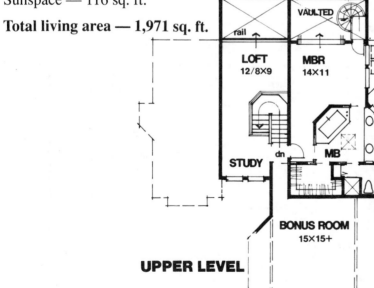

UPPER LEVEL

Three-bedroom with Space to Grow

No. 91425

This contemporary design with a hint of traditional detailing has a spacious covered entry that leads into a vaulted foyer, accented with a large clerestory window. Adjacent to the vaulted family room is the island kitchen which is brightened by a lightwell. Accesssible from the master bedroom, the solar greenhouse, which is equipped with a built-in hot tub, admits sunlight and warmth to an adjoining bath and family room. The master bedroom features a vaulted ceiling, two walk-in closets and a privacy deck. The library on the second level provides space for a wood-burning stove. An optional, unfinished bonus room is located over the garage with an arched accent window as a focal point. Basement option available, please specify when ordering.

First floor — 1,709 sq. ft.
Second floor — 789 sq. ft.
Bonus room — 336 sq. ft.
Garage — 2-car

Total living area — 2,498 sq. ft

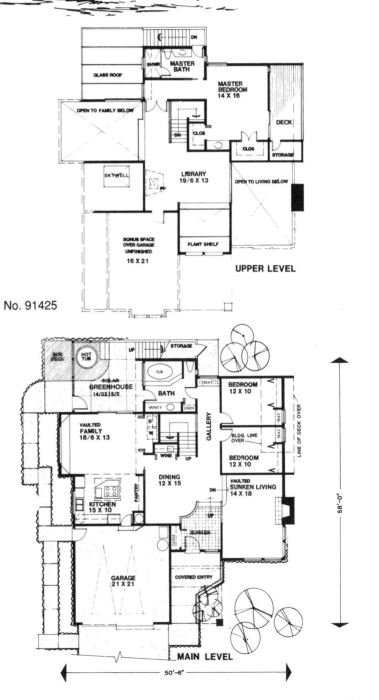

No. 91425

Built-In Bonus

No. 91616

Here's a sun-drenched beauty you'll love coming home to. The curving staircase that dominates the towering, skylit foyer is mirrored in the rounded, two-story window wall in the adjoining living room. Past the pantry, utility, and powder rooms, you'll find informal areas overlooking the backyard, separated by columns for an open feeling. The island kitchen easily serves both the glass-walled breakfast nook and bay-windowed dining room, as well as the comfortable family room with its fireplace flanked by windows and plant shelves. Upstairs, skylights, bay windows, and distinctive ceiling treatments give every room a unique personality. A hall bath serves the kids' rooms, but the master suite enjoys a private, skylit bath with every amenity.

First floor — 1,762 sq. ft.
Second floor — 1,178 sq. ft.
Bonus room — 121 sq. ft.
Garage — 3-car

Total living area — 2,940 sq. ft.

UPPER FLOOR

No. 91616

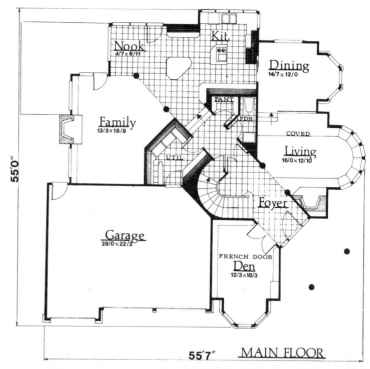

MAIN FLOOR

Savor the Sunshine

No. 91512

The imposing facade of this gracious, brick-accented home hints at the dramatic plan you'll find inside. From the towering-entry foyer dominated by a curving staircase to the flowing openness of formal and family areas, this is a home with a spacious feeling. Notice the abundant windows that let the sun shine into every room, and the soaring, vaulted ceilings of the living room and the well-appointed master suite. And, there's built-in convenience everywhere: a rangetop island and walk-in pantry in the gourmet kitchen, a handy laundry room with garage access, two-and-a-half baths, and ample closet space in each bedroom.

First floor — 1,408 sq. ft.
Second floor — 1,024 sq. ft.
Garage — 3-car

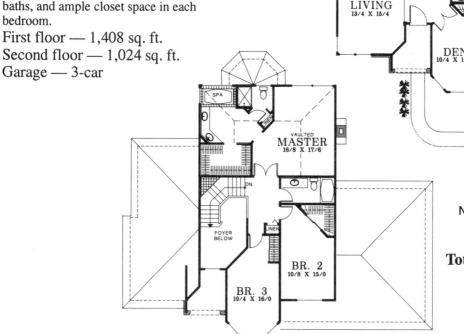

No. 91512

Total living area — 2,432 sq. ft.

Hawaii-Inspired Split-Level

No. 91717

Entry level is mid-level, with a master suite a half-story up, and utilities, guest suite, main bathroom and garage a half-story down. A laundry chute from the bathroom in the master suite on the upper level leads to the utility room on the bottom level. Ceilings are high and vaulted in all the mid-level rooms — entry, office, living room, family room and kitchen. The kitchen has plenty of extra storage available in the pantry and an eating bar built right into the food preparation island. Two bathrooms are located on the lower level. One is part of a guest suite with an extra-large closet. The master suite has skylights and features an oversized walk-in closet and double vanities in a dressing area next to a large spa.

First floor — 1,742 sq. ft.
Second floor — 640 sq. ft.
Garage — 629 sq. ft.

Total living area — 2,382 sq. ft.

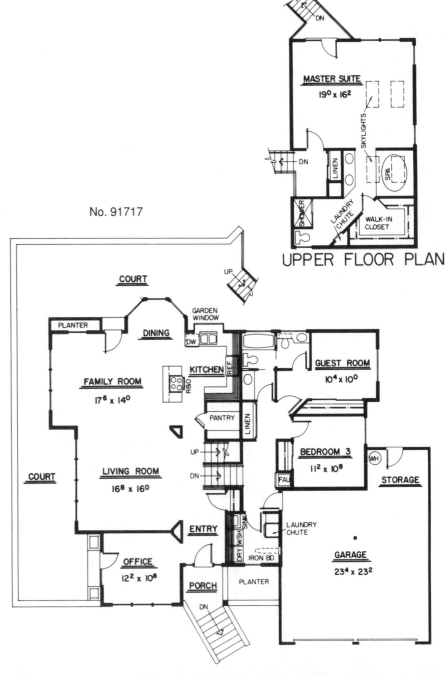

No. 91717

UPPER FLOOR PLAN

MASTER SUITE
19^0 x 16^2

GUEST ROOM
10^4 x 10^0

FAMILY ROOM
17^6 x 14^0

LIVING ROOM
16^8 x 16^0

BEDROOM 3
11^2 x 10^8

OFFICE
12^2 x 10^8

GARAGE
23^4 x 23^2

Life In The Round

No. 99230

Curves and circular spaces are abound for a unique living space. The entire second floor is devoted to an exquisite master suite, with semi-circular bay, bath suite with a skylight, and whirlpool. Descend the sweeping staircase to enter the gracious gathering room, with a three-story window tower at the far end and an open fireplace that warms the adjoining study. The first-floor bedroom has a balcony walk-out to the terrace. The circular theme is continued in the kitchen, which opens to a perfectly round breakfast room, with an abundance of windows. Every bath in the house is designed for unexpected space. The finished lower level adds a substantial feel of quality and luxury to this elegant home. Here, you'll find a curving wetbar, huge exercise room with a mirrored wall, round hot tub, and adjoining sauna and full bath. The activities room is spacious enough for nearly any pastime, and is finished off with a three-story window tower.

First floor — 1,570 sq. ft.

Second floor — 598 sq. ft.

Lower level — 1,570 sq. ft.

Garage — 462 sq. ft. & storage

Total living area — 3,738 sq. ft.

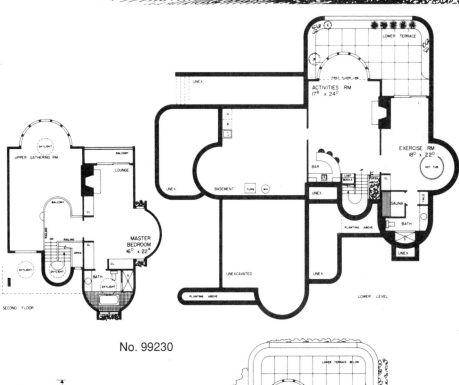

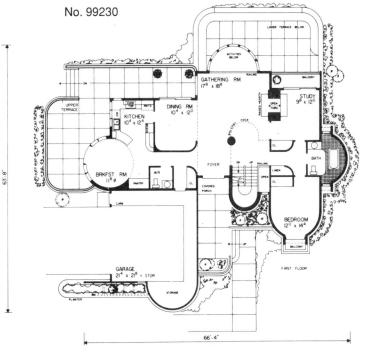

No. 99230

Stucco Splendor

No. 91613

Massive stucco columns combine with floor-to-ceiling glass walls to create a fascinating home you'll be proud to own. The impressive foyer affords a view of the cozy den with adjoining full bath, the fireplaced living room that flows into the dining room, and the balcony overhead that links three bedrooms and two skylit baths. Step through the center hallway to family areas at the rear of the house, where the island kitchen, glass-walled nook, and fireplaced family room with wetbar share the backyard view. Reach the upper levels on the elegant staircase that arcs over the foyer, or the U-shaped staircase off the kitchen. The enchanting master suite features a private sitting room, fabulous spa bath, and walk-in closet. There's even a bonus room over the garage.

First floor — 2,268 sq. ft.
Second floor — 1,484 sq. ft.
Bonus — 300 sq. ft.
Garage — 3-car

Total living area — 4,052 sq. ft.

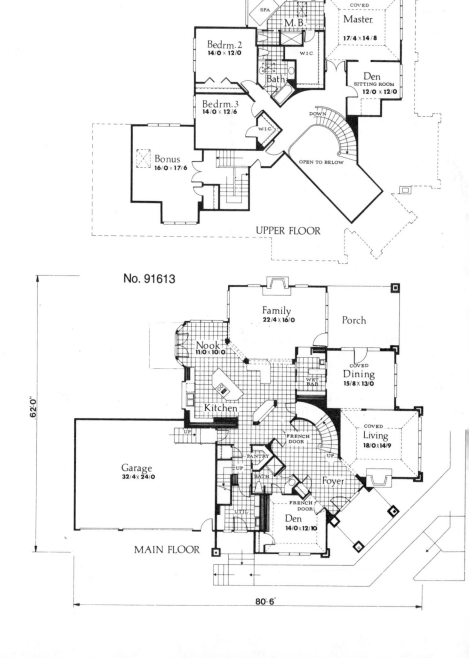

UPPER FLOOR

MAIN FLOOR

Windows And Angles Create Spectacular Views

No. 91655

This splendid, contemporary home makes creative use of a unique floor plan. From the imposing front with large windows and stunning stucco exterior, to the dramatic coved-ceilings and angular rooms, it's a dream come true. Luxuriate in the spa in the master suite or enjoy views from magnificent windows in the family and living rooms, dining nook and master bedroom.

Main floor — 1,173 sq. ft.
Upper floor — 823 sq. ft.
Bonus room — 204 sq. ft.
Garage — 2-car

Total living area — 1,996 sq. ft.

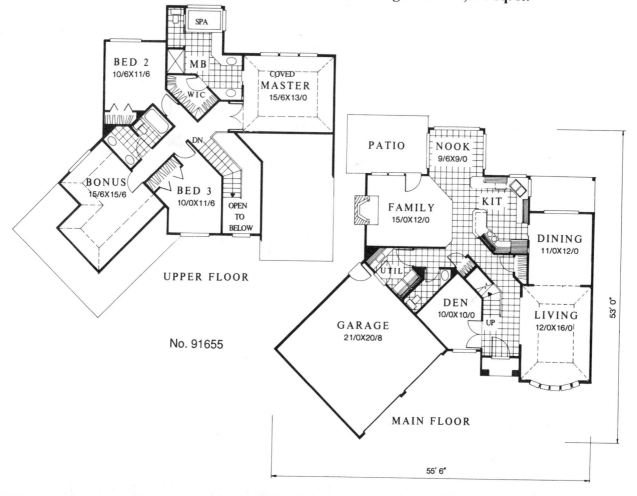

No. 91655

Daytime Delight

No. 91607

This exquisite, carefree home will be bathed in sunlight from dawn to dusk. The central foyer opens to a large, vaulted living and dining room arrangement that flows together for an open feeling accentuated by huge windows. French doors lend a quiet atmosphere to the front-facing den or bedroom off the foyer. You'll find two more bedrooms and two full baths just around the corner, past the utility room. Notice the exciting master suite with its vaulted ceiling and private double-vanitied bath. Informal areas overlooking the backyard include the soaring family room crowned by a fireplace, a glass-walled dining nook with access to a covered porch, and a kitchen that's centrally located for maximum convenience.

Main living area — 1,653 sq. ft.
Garage — 2-car

Total living area — 1,653 sq. ft.

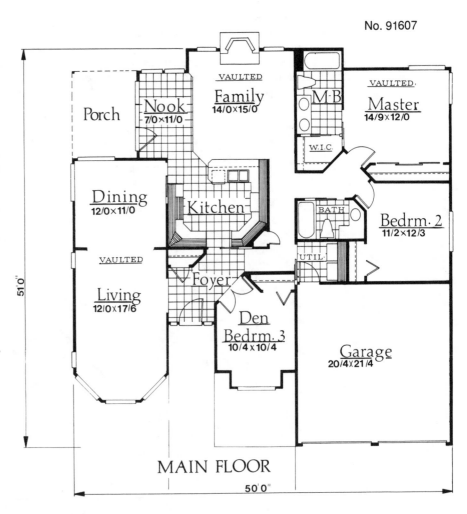

No. 91607

MAIN FLOOR

Hillside Home Is Perfect for Parties

No. 10585

It won't matter if it rains on your barbecue, you can retreat to the gazebo or covered patio. Inside, entertain your guests in the Great room or recreation room. Both are equipped with wetbars for maximum convenience. Traffic moves smoothly throughout the upper level, which features an island kitchen, a buffet counter in the morning room and double doors into the formal dining room. Gain access to the deck from the great room or master bedroom with full bath. On the lower level, there's plenty of storage space, along with two bedrooms, 1-1/2 baths, and an office.

First floor — 2,647 sq. ft.
Basement/finished area — 2,108 sq. ft.
Basement/unfinished area — 807 sq. ft.
Garage — 807 sq. ft.
Covered porch — 128 sq. ft.

Total living area — 4,755 sq. ft.

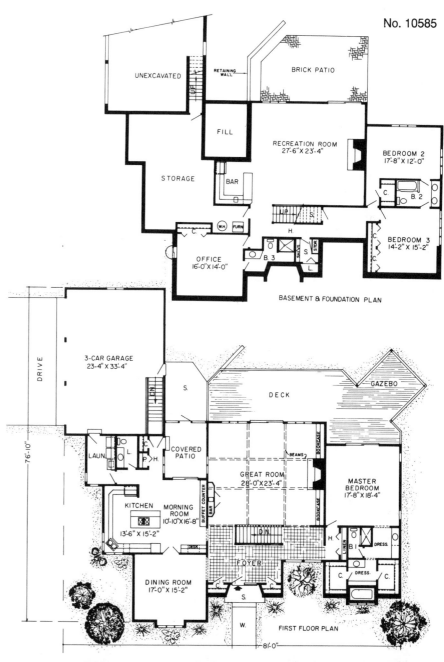

No. 10585

BASEMENT & FOUNDATION PLAN

FIRST FLOOR PLAN

Practical, Yet Pretty

No. 91511

Here's a sturdy brick beauty full of exciting angles and practical features. Notice the dramatic vaulted ceilings in the fireplaced living room, formal dining room, and front-facing bedroom upstairs. Down-to-earth design elements include a well-appointed island kitchen, located just steps away from the formal dining room, fireplaced family room, and bay-windowed breakfast nook. Don't miss the first-floor bedroom just around the corner from the powder room. As you walk upstairs, you'll feel the natural warmth from the skylight overhead. The hall bath serves the front bedrooms and the bonus room over the garage. But the vaulted master suite boasts a private, skylit bath with every amenity.

First floor — 1,462 sq. ft.
Second floor — 1,013 sq. ft.
Bonus Room — 180 sq. ft.
Garage — 2-car

Total living area — 2,475 sq. ft.

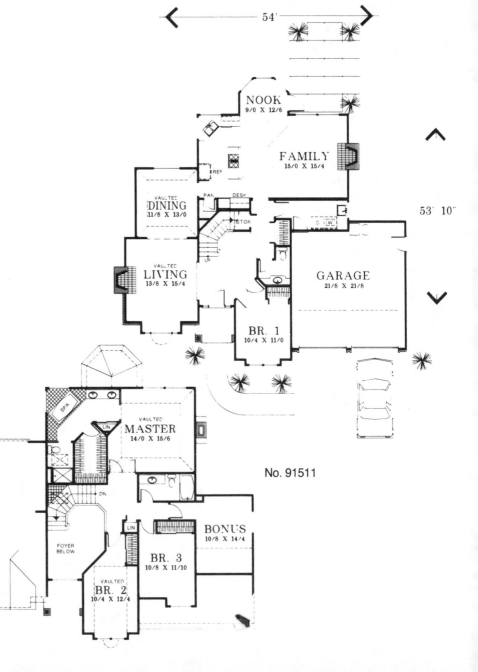

No. 91511

Compact Gem Features Stunning Views

No. 90389

Need a compact plan with high energy impact? Here's the house for you! Standing in the entry flooded with light from a half-round window high overhead, you'll be treated to an impressive view of active areas and the second-floor balcony. Step up to the sunny family room, which features a fireplace and a built-in bar. The galley kitchen between family and formal living areas is convenient no matter where you're serving dinner: in the stunning, vaulted Great room, breakfast bay, or the rear deck. An open stairway leads to the sleeping floor, where three bedrooms and two full baths insure early morning convenience for your busy family.

First floor — 922 sq. ft.
Second floor — 802 sq. ft.

Total living area — 1,724 sq. ft.

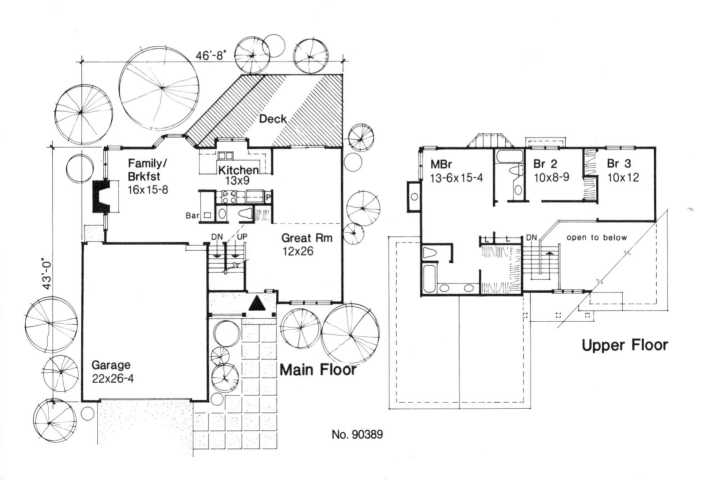

No. 90389

Comtemporary with Class

No 91426

This home, with the exciting look of wood, is a Northwest comtemporary. It is shown finished in cedar siding with wood shakes. The Great room, featuring a 9 foot high ceiling with decorative beams has a wood stove and is open to the kitchen and breakfast room. The vaulted foyer has visual access to the second floor balcony. A walk-through utility and pantry closet lies between the garage and the foyer. The master bedroom, separated from the other bedrooms, has a large walk-in closet, double-vanitied bath, and private access to the deck.

First floor — 1,686 sq. ft.
Second floor — 674 sq. ft.
Garage — 2-car

Total living area — 2,360 sq. ft.

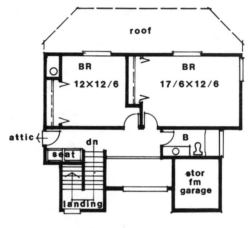

UPPER LEVEL

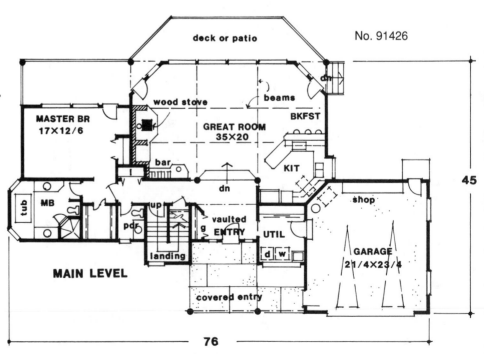

No. 91426

MAIN LEVEL

Contemporary Energy-Saver

No. 91402

Abundant windows, soaring ceilings, and a generous sprinkling of skylights lend a contemporary flavor to this updated Cape Cod plan. Traditional touches include a central staircase, two cozy first-floor bedrooms, and two full baths. But, the balcony view from the loft, the dramatic living room dominated by a huge arched window, and the skylit kitchen that opens to the family-dining room are strictly contemporary. The open plan makes maximum use of the energy-saving wood stove between the living and family rooms. For even greater savings, add the optional sunspace. Specify a crawlspace or full basement when ordering this plan.

First floor — 1,154 sq. ft.
Second floor — 585 sq. ft.
Garage — 516 sq. ft.

Total living area — 1,739 sq. ft.

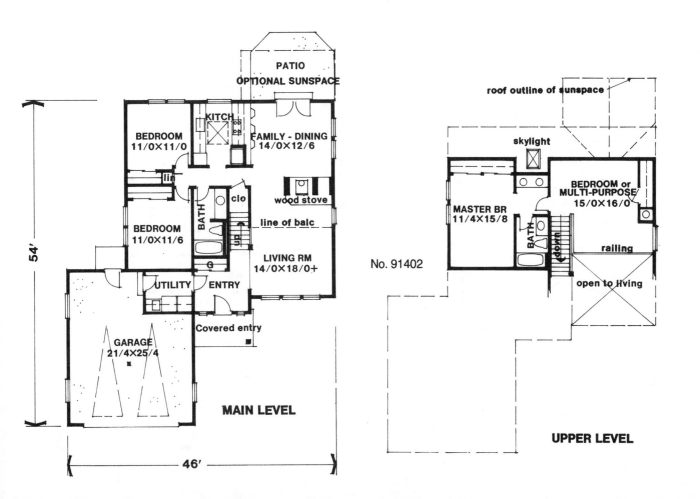

Infinite Possibilities

No. 91424

Graceful arches adorn the facade of this distinctive three-bedroom home. Step from the covered porch into a dramatic vaulted entry that opens to a soaring, fireplaced living room with an arched floor-to-ceiling window. The adjoining dining room and handy powder room nearby complete this very elegant, exciting area that's ideal for entertaining. You'll find a comfortable, informal family room, kitchen and sunny eating nook at the rear of the house. Have the kids pull a stool up to the kitchen peninsula for their afternoon snacks. Up the skylit staircase, three bedrooms and two baths include the vaulted master suite with garden tub and twin walk-in closets. The bonus room over the garage offers lots of exciting possibilities.

First floor — 1,290 sq. ft.
Second floor — 932 sq. ft.
Bonus room — 228 sq. ft.
Garage — 2-car

Total living area — 2,450 sq. ft.

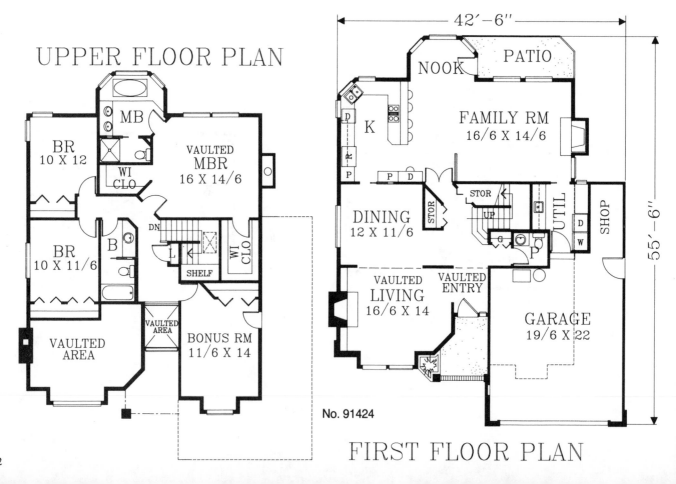

UPPER FLOOR PLAN

FIRST FLOOR PLAN

No. 91424

Soaring Roof Lines Hint at Dramatic Interior

No. 91405

From the vaulted living room to the bayed master bath, every room in this three-bedroom beauty features interesting angles. The spacious,

living-dining room arrangement at the front of the house is steps away from the kitchen. Three corner windows lend a greenhouse feeling to this well-appointed room, which opens to the informal dining bay and fireplaced family room. An elegant, U-shaped staircase leads to sleeping areas, tucked upstairs for a quiet atmosphere. There are lots of options in this intriguing

home, including a bonus room over the garage if you need the space. Specify a crawlspace or basement when ordering this plan.

First floor — 1,162 sq. ft.
Second floor — 807 sq. ft.
Garage — 446 sq. ft.

Total living area — 1,969 sq. ft.

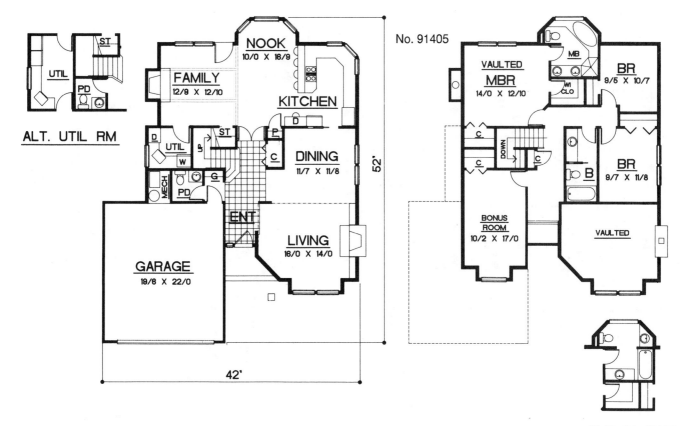

No. 91405

ALT. UTIL RM

ALT. M. BATH

Use the Deck off the Master Suite for Private Sunbaths

No. 91411

Orient this charming sun-catcher to the south, add the optional sunspace off the dining room, and you'll have a solar home without equal. The sunken living room, formal dining room, and island kitchen with adjoining, informal nook all enjoy an expansive view of the patio and backyard beyond. A fireplace in the living room, and a wood stove separating the nook and family room keep the house toasty when the sun goes down. The sunny atmosphere found on the first floor continues upstairs, where skylights brighten the balcony and master bath. With three bedrooms on the upper floor, and one downstairs, you can promise the kids their own rooms. Specify crawlspace or basement when ordering this plan.

First floor — 1,249 sq. ft.
Second floor — 890 sq. ft.
Garage — 462 sq. ft.

Total living area — 2,139 sq. ft.

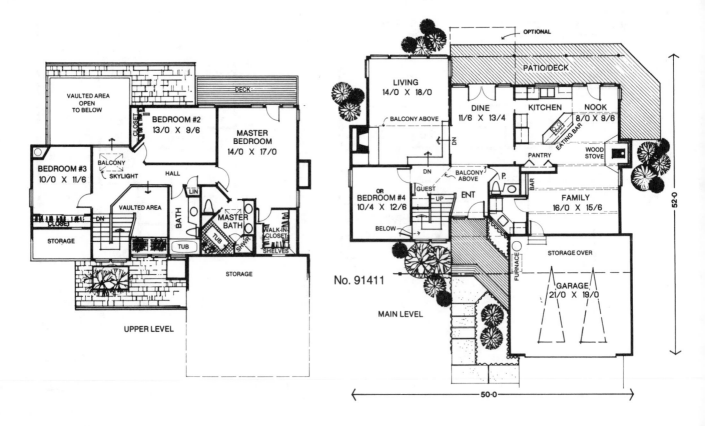

Design Incorporates Informal and Formal

No. 90317

The main level of this two-story home is divided into formal and informal living areas by the central placement of the staircase and the kitchen. The two-story living room and the dining room with its unique bump-out window are located to one side of the home. On the other side are the family room with its inviting fireplace and the breakfast room which has sliding glass doors onto the deck. Four bedrooms comprise the second floor. The expansive master bedroom features a five-piece bath and two walk-in closets.

Main level — 1,413 sq. ft.
Upper level — 1,245 sq. ft.
Basement — 1,413 sq. ft.
Garage — 689 sq. ft.

Total living area — 2,658 sq. ft.

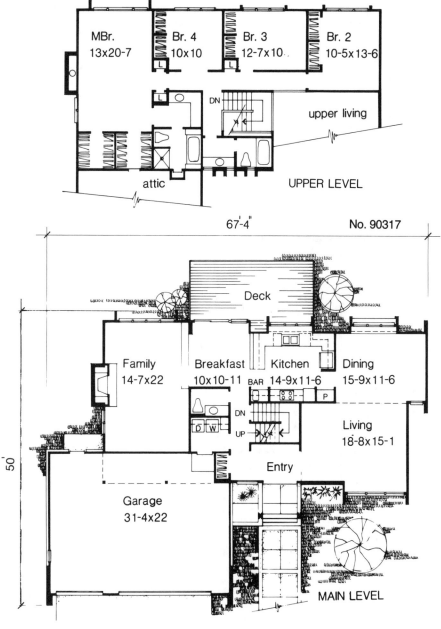

MBr. 13x20-7   Br. 4 10x10   Br. 3 12-7x10   Br. 2 10-5x13-6

DN

upper living

attic

UPPER LEVEL

67'-4"   No. 90317

50'

Deck

Family 14-7x22   Breakfast 10x10-11   Kitchen 14-9x11-6   Dining 15-9x11-6

BAR

DN   UP

D W

Living 18-8x15-1

Entry

Garage 31-4x22

MAIN LEVEL

Vertical Siding Adds Contemporary Appeal

No. 91407

Here's a traditional family home with a contemporary flavor. The entry is flanked by the dramatic, vaulted living room and a cozy den that doubles as a guest room. Informal areas at the rear of the house command an expansive view of the backyard, thanks to windows on three sides. The unique, open arrangement of the rangetop island kitchen, dining bay, and fireplaced family room keeps the cook from getting lonely. The U-shaped stairs, just across from the handy powder room, lead to a balcony linking three bedrooms. You'll love the master suite, which features a luxurious sunken tub with a view. Need more room? Finish the optional bonus space over the garage. Specify a crawlspace or basement when ordering this plan.

First floor — 1,153 sq. ft.
Second floor — 787 sq. ft.
Garage — 537 sq. ft.

Total living area —1,940 sq. ft.

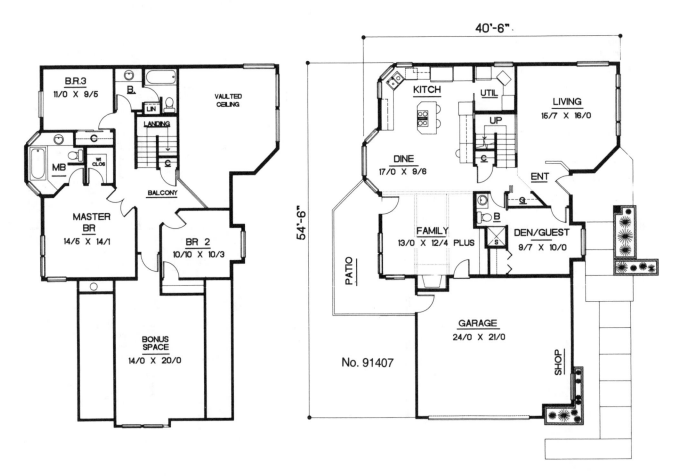

Lots of Space in this Small Package

No. 90378

Here's a compact gem that won't break your budget. Well-placed windows, an open plan, and vaulted ceilings lend a spacious feeling to this contemporary home. The dynamic, soaring angles of the living room are accentuated by the fireplace that dominates the room. Eat in the dining room adjoining the kitchen, or step through the sliders for dinner on the deck. And, when it's time to make coffee in the morning, you'll love the first-floor location of the master suite, just steps away from the kitchen. Upstairs, a full bath serves two bedrooms, each with a walk-in closet.

First floor — 878 sq. ft.
Second floor — 405 sq. ft.
Garage — 2-car

Total living area — 1,283 sq. ft.

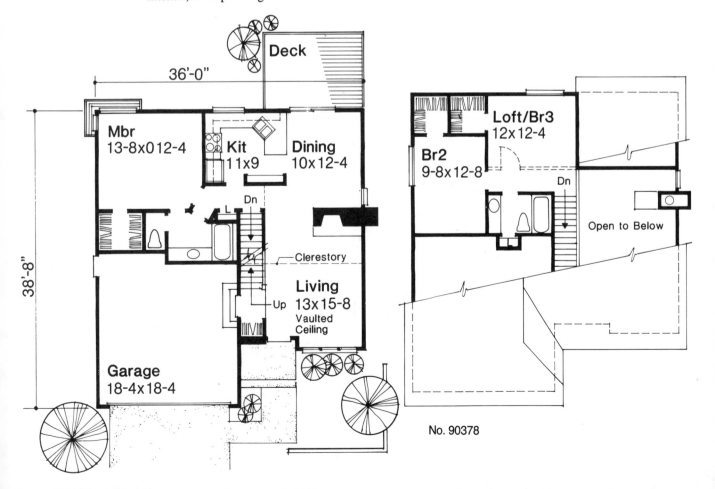

No. 90378

Sunny and Spacious

No. 91406

Step into the entry and glance into the two-story, fireplaced living room that sets the stage for this dramatic plan. Here's an exceptional spot for entertaining, with a handy powder room and guest room just steps away. You'll find an efficient, island kitchen, bayed dining room, and cozy, beamed family room that flow together in one appealing space at the rear of the house. Upstairs, you'll find three ample bedrooms, including the elegant master suite tucked behind double doors. An optional bonus room gives you plenty of room for your growing family. Be sure to specify a crawlspace or basement when ordering this plan.

First floor — 1,140 sq. ft.
Second floor — 845 sq. ft.
Garage — 440 sq. ft.

No. 91406

42'

DINE
9/10 X 18/10

KITCH

FAMILY
12/8X14/8

UTIL

PTY

UP

PWD

LIVING RM
18/0X14/0

ENTRY

DEN/GUEST
15/2X9/8

GARAGE
19/7X21/10

MAIN FLOOR PLAN

ALT MASTER BATH

BEDROOM
9/8X11/0

M.BATH

MASTER BR
14/0X14/4

WI CLO

BATH

DOWN

BEDROOM
12/0 X 12/6

VAULTED LIVING RM
BELOW

OPTIONAL
BONUS RM
13/2X11/8

STORAGE

UPPER FLOOR PLAN

UP

DN

ALT. PLAN W/ BSMT

Total living area — 1,985 sq. ft.

Built In Drama

No. 91513

This contemporary plan in a clapboard package is loaded with dramatic sizzle generally found only in larger homes. Stand on the second-floor balcony for a view of the two-story nook and foyer in one sweeping glance. Four bedrooms,

two luxury baths with double vanities, and a practical laundry room complete the upper floor. The first floor is just as exciting, with a two-story view from the nook, a sunken family room with corner window arrangement and a toasty fireplace, and the adjoining living and dining room combination separated by a single step and an open

railing. The kitchen, with its rangetop island and built-in conveniences, is the gourmet's dream you've always wanted.

First floor — 1,150 sq. ft.
Second floor — 1,150 sq. ft.
Garage — 2-car

Total living area — 2,300 sq. ft.

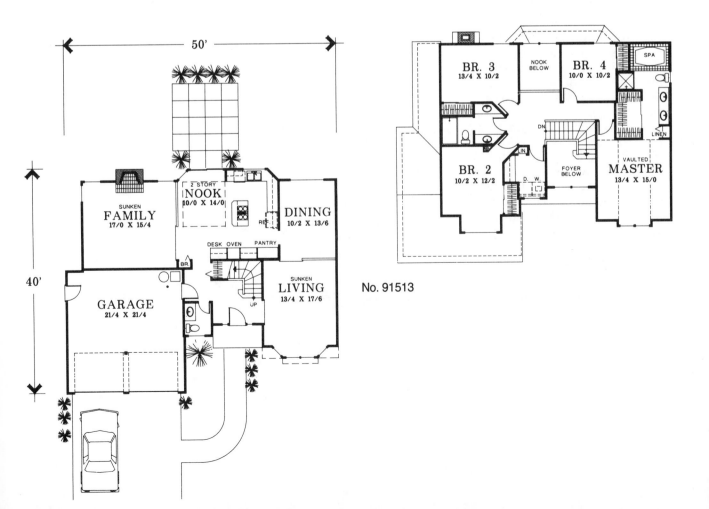

No. 91513

Master Suite Features Private Deck

No. 91404

Here's an elegant contemporary with a style all its own. The covered entry leads to a central foyer accessible to every area of the house. Surrounded by a two-story bay window, the curving stairway leads to three bedrooms, two full baths, and a sweeping view of the Great room and kitchen below. Walk straight ahead to the sunken Great room, a celebration of light and space united with the great outdoors by three magnificent window walls. With three appealing dining spots—a sunny nook adjoining the kitchen, the bayed, formal dining room, or the expansive deck—mealtimes will always be interesting. And, when you're looking for a quiet spot, retreat to the den tucked behind the garage. Specify a crawlspace or full basement when ordering this plan.

First floor — 1,550 sq. ft.
Second floor — 1,001 sq. ft.
Garage — 750 sq. ft.

Total living area — 2,551 sq. ft.

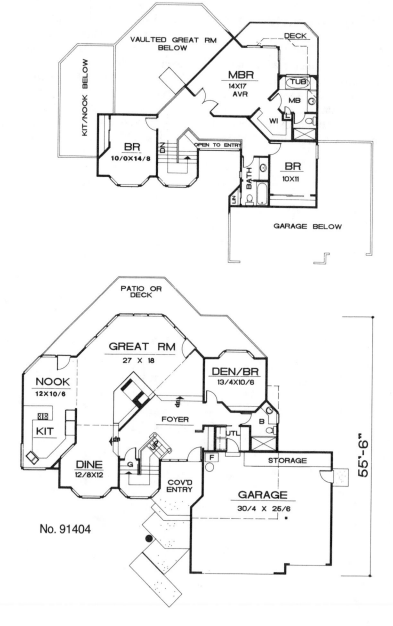

No. 91404

Open Space Characterizes Compact Plan

No. 90386

A vaulted entry, lit from above by a double window, provides an impressive introduction to this distinctive family home. The excitement continues as you proceed into the soaring living room and adjoining dining room, set apart from family areas for elegant entertaining. At the rear of the house, the country kitchen features a cozy fireplace, a bay window just perfect for your kitchen table, and access to a rear deck. The natural light present in the entry illuminates the stairwell through a half-round window that's beautiful from both interior and exterior perspectives. Three bedrooms and two full baths include the dramatically vaulted master suite at the rear of the house.

First floor — 928 sq. ft.
Second floor — 907 sq. ft.
Garage — 2-car

Total living area — 1,835 sq. ft.

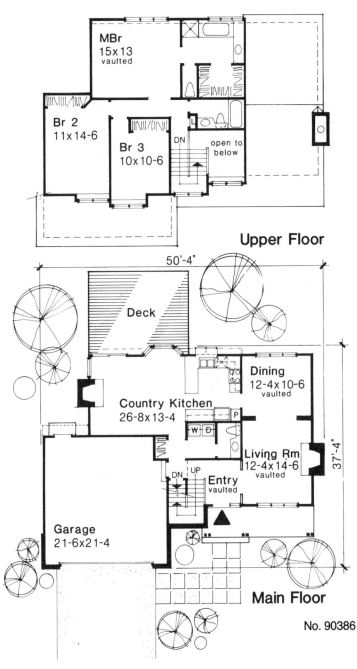

Upper Floor

Main Floor

No. 90386

Create a Dramatic Impression

No. 91400

Soaring roof lines and loads of glass add interior and exterior excitement to this beautiful, three or four-bedroom contemporary. See all the active areas in one sweeping glance from the two-story entry. This plan eliminates unnecessary walls, so the island kitchen, dining room, and vaulted, sunken Great room unite for a spacious feeling. A huge, wrap-around deck adds warm weather living space. Add the optional sunspace for year-round enjoyment. Two first-floor bedrooms feature built-in desks, and easy access to a full bath. The second-floor balcony overlooking the Great room leads to the luxurious master suite with adjoining skylit bath. Specify a crawlspace or full basement when ordering this plan.

First floor — 1,450 sq. ft.
Second floor — 650 sq. ft.
Garage — 558 sq. ft.

Total living area — 2,100 sq. ft.

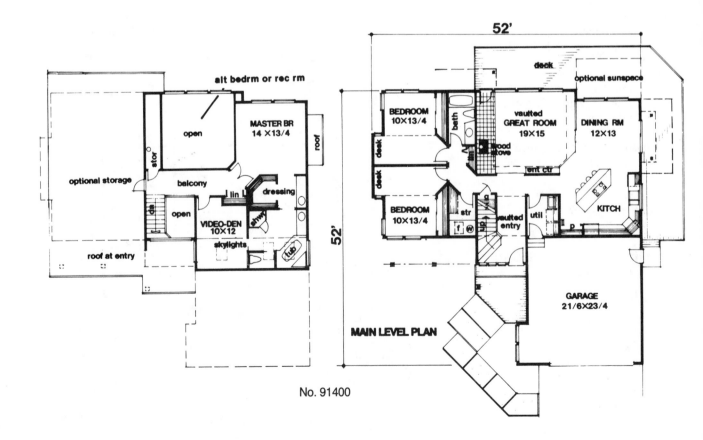

No. 91400

Open Design Creates Spacious Feeling

No. 90925

Looking for just the right plan for that hillside lot? Here's a design that will fit a smaller lot with a front-to-back or a side-to-side slope. Vaulted ceilings and lots of glass brighten the living areas, arranged to afford a view to the street. The large kitchen and breakfast nook overlook a cozy family room, which opens out onto an attractive patio. Up a short flight of stairs are three roomy bedrooms and family bath. The master suite has its own bathroom, a wall of mirrored closets for dressing and a beautiful vaulted ceiling with clerestory windows overhead.

Lower floor — 1,118 sq. ft.
Upper floor — 688 sq. ft.
Unfinished basement — 380 sq. ft.
Garage — 430 sq. ft.
Width — 40'-0"
Depth — 37'-0"

Total living area — 1,806 sq. ft.

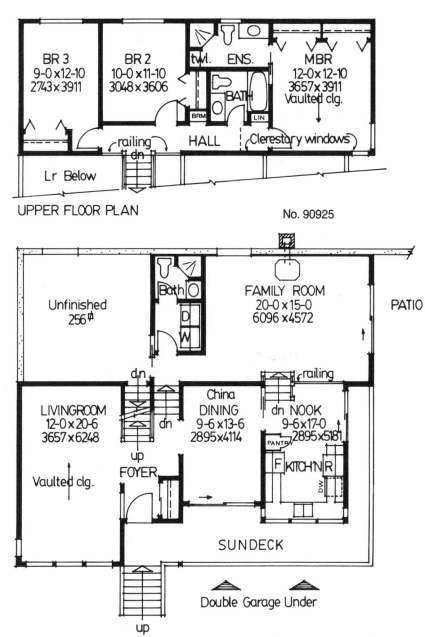

Double Decks Adorn Luxurious Master Suite

No. 91022

Curves soften the exterior and interior spaces of this dramatic contemporary designed for sun worshippers. Abundant windows, indoor planters and three decks unite every room with the great outdoors. Steps and railings divide active areas without compromising the home's airy feeling. When the sun goes down, enjoy the warmth of the fireplace in the living and dining rooms or the wood stove in the family room. Main floor bedrooms, adjacent to a convenient full bath, are tucked away from family areas for quiet bedtimes. The master suite upstairs is a wonderful retreat you're sure to enjoy. Please specify basement, slab or crawlspace foundation when ordering.

Main floor — 1,985 sq. ft.
Upper floor — 715 sq. ft.

Total living area —2,700 sq. ft.

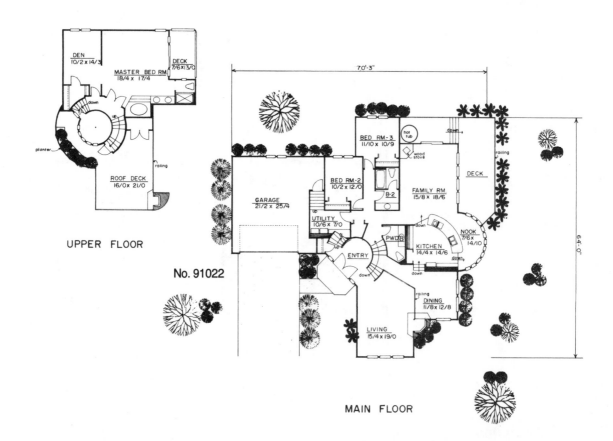

UPPER FLOOR

No. 91022

MAIN FLOOR

Celebration of Light and Space

No. 91212

Vertical and diagonal siding reinforce the soaring roof lines of this dramatic contemporary. And inside, the excitement of open space and lots of glass insures a sunny atmosphere in any weather. When the sun goes down, the massive fireplace dominating the Great room will add a cozy glow. The cook will never be lonely in the efficient island kitchen that easily serves the breakfast bar or the dining room table overlooking the trellised deck. Large vertical windows and generous closets characterize the three cheerful bedrooms tucked into a private wing.

And, look at the sunroom that encloses the tub in the master suite. There's a lot of luxury in this compact home! No materials list available for this plan.

Main living area — 1,873 sq. ft.
Garage — 467 sq. ft.

Total living area — 1,873 sq. ft.

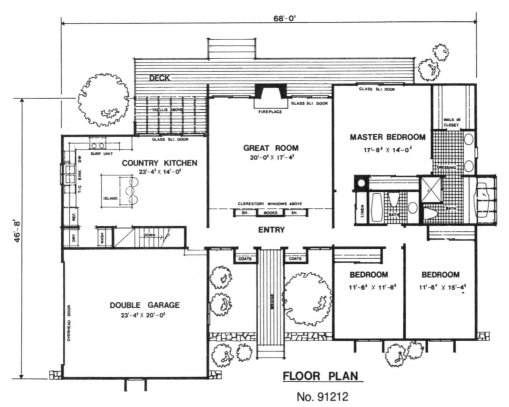

FLOOR PLAN
No. 91212

No materials list available

Indoor-Outdoor Unity

No. 91011

One-level living has never been more interesting than in this three-bedroom home with attached three-car garage. From the protected entry, the central foyer leads down the hall to the bedroom wing, into the formal living areas, or into the sun-washed library. At the end of the bedroom hall, you'll find a luxurious master suite, complete with spa and a private deck. Straight ahead, glass walls and an open plan unite the formal dining and sunken living rooms with the back yard. The adjoining island kitchen, nook, and family room continue the outdoor feeling with expansive windows and sliders to the surrounding covered patio.

Main living area — 2,242 sq. ft.

Total living area — 2,242 sq. ft.

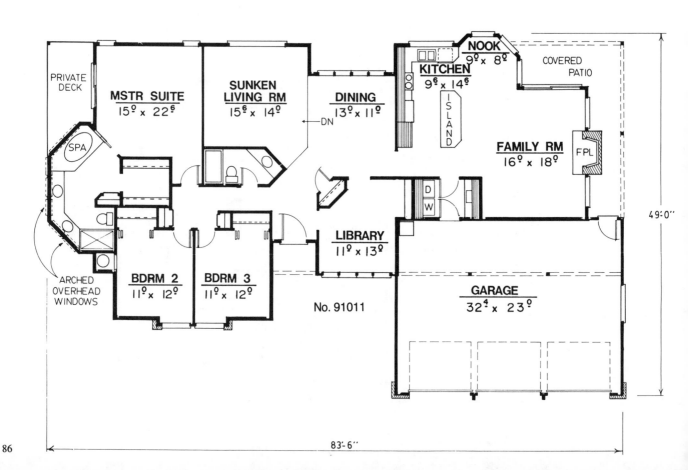

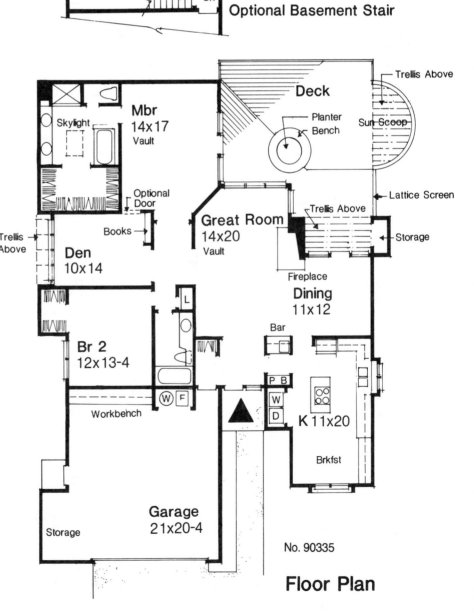

Optional Basement Stair

Efficient Single Level Design

No. 90335

All the conveniences one enjoys and expects are present in this step-saving single level plan. A very large kitchen offers a popular center island with built-in range to speed food preparation. The breakfast room is charming and well lighted by two-level windows. The dining room sports a wetbar, while the great room is distinguished by a vaulted ceiling and a corner fireplace. The master bedroom is set off by a very large bath area with a skylight and an exit to the deck.

Main living area — 1,700 sq. ft.

Total living area — 1,700 sq. ft.

No. 90335

Floor Plan

Energy Efficient Single Level

No. 91744

Energy efficiency is the primary concern in this plan. Windows, high and low, make up most of the rear walls of the family room creating a bright environment. In fact, most of the rooms have enough light to make daytime electricity almost obsolete.

The airlock entryway opens to a large dining room and living room. The kitchen has a central work island and is open to the vaulted family room. The master suite has a personal bath with double vanity and opens onto a deck outside. Two smaller bedrooms share a full bath at the opposite end of the house. A pantry is placed before a utility area that leads to a two-car garage.

Main living area — 2,068 sq. ft.
Covered porch — 235 sq. ft.
Garage — 544 sq. ft.

Total living area — 2,068 sq. ft.

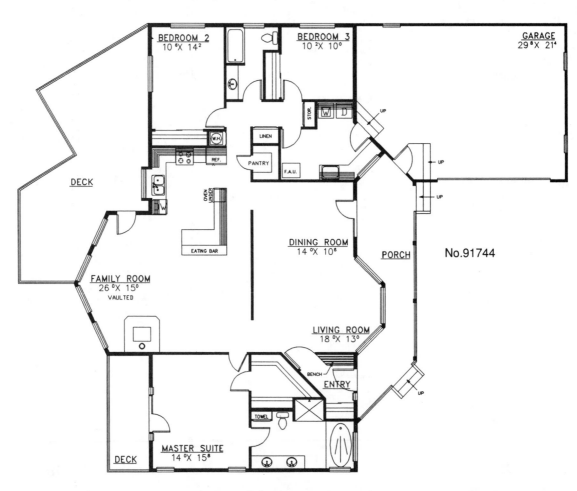

Treat Yourself to This Luxurious Retreat

No. 91705

Built with a sky-lit covered pool in its central courtyard, this plan is a recreational "cabin" type home, designed as a vacation get-away for ownership by two couples. A broad double entryway opens directly onto the pool area. In fact, it's necessary to reenter the pool room in order to move from any one area of the house to another but at the same time, all rooms can be closed off from it. The living room takes access a step further with two sets of sliding glass doors which can be left open for entertaining. Outward-facing windows ring the five-sided vaulted-Great room. Four skylights add to the flood of natural light. A large utility room, with pantry, is located near the garage for easy access. Additional storage is also available in the long double garage.

Main living area — 2,282 sq. ft.
Pool room — 1,086 sq. ft.
Garage — 676 sq. ft.

Total living area — 3,368 sq. ft.

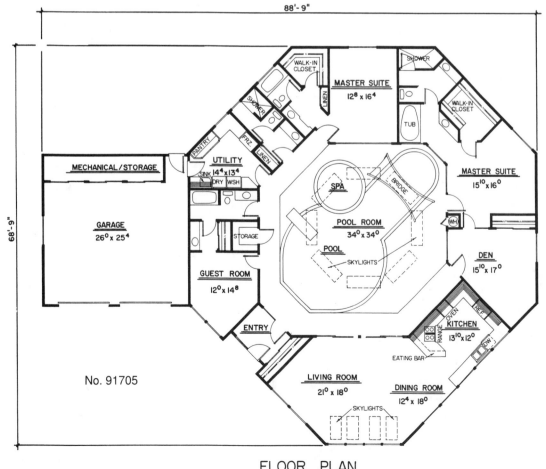

No. 91705

FLOOR PLAN

New Dimensions in Sight

No. 90348

Wherever you relax in this contemporary pleasure home, you'll enjoy the view. Climb the ladder into the top-of-the-tower sleeping loft and look out the huge fan-shaped window for a spectacular sight. Or, relax in the living room and look out the glass windows that brighten the room's corner. This home is a sightseer's paradise. The sweeping deck is accessed by the master bedroom or the living-dining area. With its open floor plan and bright interior, this spacious three-level home sleeps and entertains as many or as few as you want. For you and your fortunate guests inside, the view is everywhere.

Main living area — 1,097 sq. ft.

Total living area — 1,097 sq. ft.

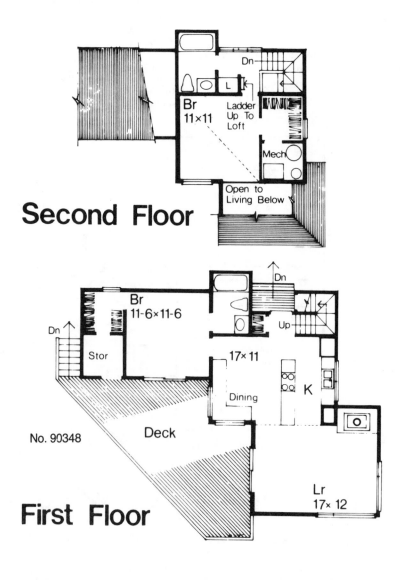

Second Floor

Br 11×11
Dn
L
Ladder Up To Loft
Mech
Open to Living Below

First Floor

No. 90348
Dn
Br 11-6×11-6
Stor
Dn
Up
17×11
Dining
K
Deck
Lr 17×12

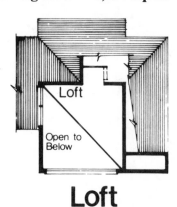

Loft
Open to Below

Loft

Let the Sun Shine In

No. 10629

This sleek contemporary is made to order for the family that loves the outdoors. The design features four decks — two upstairs and two down — along with sliding glass doors and windows galore. Entering the half-round, two-story foyer, turn left to reach the breakfast room, formal dining room, and kitchen, or walk straight to reach the staircase and lavatory. A step down brings you to the living room. Upstairs in the master suite, the skylight that shines on the foyer illuminates the room. Built-in desks make the other two bedrooms on this level ideal for studying.

First floor — 970 sq. ft.
Second floor — 955 sq. ft.
Garage — 573 sq. ft.

Total living area — 1,925 sq. ft.

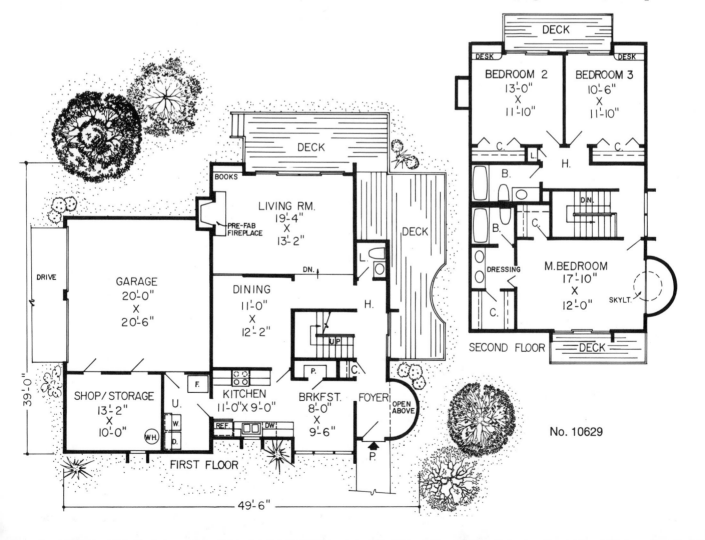

Family Living, Contemporary Style

No. 90628

Convenient living space surrounds the spacious foyer of this compact contemporary. An L-shaped stairway leads to four bedrooms and two baths on the second floor. But on the main level, active family life is the main focus. Gain easy access to both patio and garage from the open kitchen/dinette, which spills into the family room. Rainy weather shouldn't be a problem for the kids; they can play under the covered porch off the living room.

First floor — 988 sq. ft.
Second floor — 936 sq. ft.
(optional slab construction available)

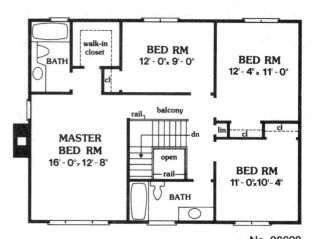

Total living area —1,924 sq. ft.

No. 90628

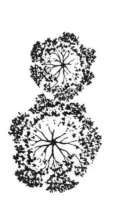

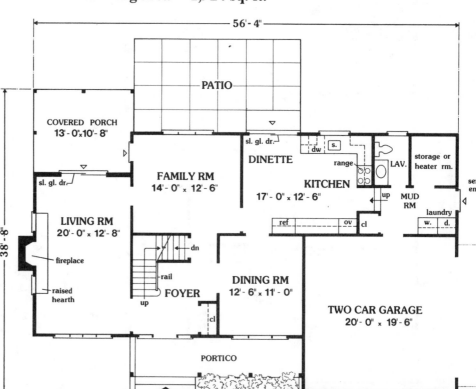

Rear of Home as Attractive as Front

No. 90413

The rear of this contemporary home features a massive stone fireplace and a full length deck which make it ideal for a mountain, golf course, lake, or other location where both the front and rear are visible. Sliding glass doors in the family room and breakfast nook open onto the deck. The modified A-frame design combines a cathedral ceiling over the sunken family room with a large studio over the two front bedrooms. An isolated master suite features a walk-in closet and compartmentalized bath with double vanity and linen closet. The front bedrooms include ample closet space and share a unique bath-and-a-half arrangement. On one side of the U-

shaped kitchen and breakfast nook is the formal dining room which opens onto the foyer. On the other side is a utility room which can be entered from either the kitchen or garage. The exterior features a massive stone fireplace, large glass areas, and a combination of vertical wood siding and stone.

First floor — 2,192 sq. ft.
Second floor — 248 sq. ft.
Basement — 2,192 sq. ft.

Total living area — 2,440 sq. ft.

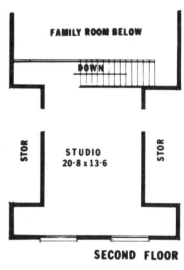

SECOND FLOOR

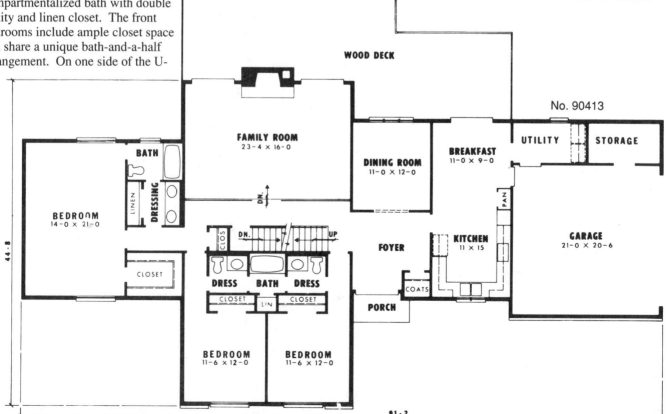

Twin Fireplaces Add Traditional Warmth

No. 90558

Gentle arches add curbside appeal to this traditional gem, characterized by a sunny atmosphere and attention to the family's need for privacy. Look at all the handy retreats in this beautiful home: the bayed sitting room off the master suite, the cozy window seat in the front bedroom, and the quiet study just off the entry. But, there's plenty of room for interaction, too, in the window-studded family areas at the rear of the house, and the living and dining rooms that flow together for a wide-open feeling. Notice the step-saving features designed into this plan: the range-top island kitchen with built-in pantry, the double-vanitied, skylit baths that serve the upstairs bedrooms, and the first-floor bath for the convenience of your guests.

First floor — 1,460 sq. ft.
Second floor — 1,005 sq. ft.
Garage — 2-car

Total living area — 2,465 sq. ft.

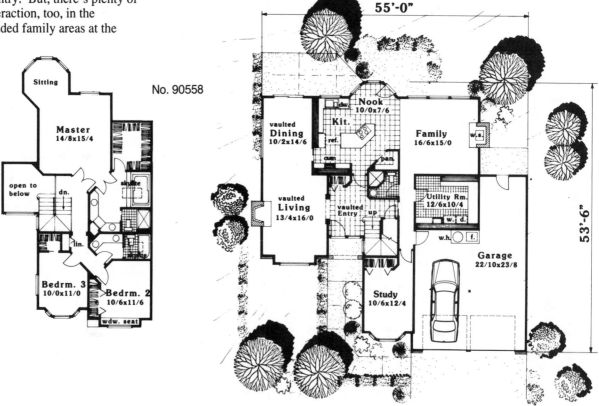

No. 90558

Sunlight Floods Every Room

No. 90511

Walk into the two-story foyer from the garage or sheltered front entry and you'll be struck by the wide-open spaciousness of this compact home. The kitchen is flanked by vaulted living and dining rooms on one side and a fireplaced family room and breakfast nook on the other. Atop the open stairs, the plush master bedroom suite lies behind double doors. Two additional bedrooms share an adjoining full bath.

First floor — 1,078 sq. ft.
Second floor — 974 sq. ft.
Garage — 2-car

Total living area — 2,052 sq. ft.

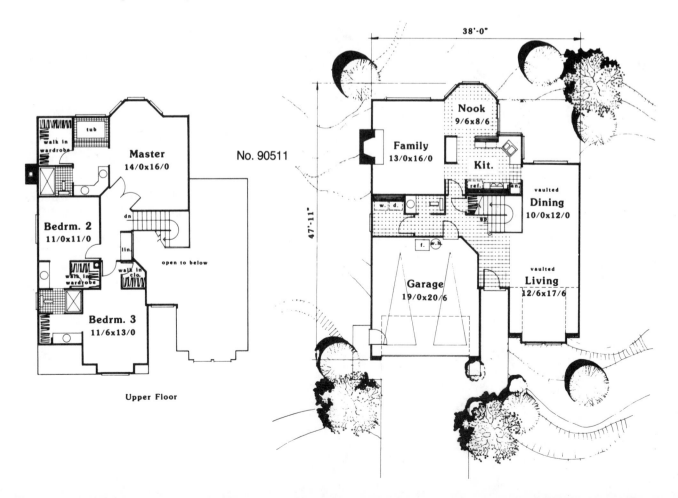

No. 90511

Upper Floor

Master
14/0x16/0

Bedrm. 2
11/0x11/0

Bedrm. 3
11/6x13/0

walk in wardrobe

tub

dn

lin.

walk in clo.

walk in wardrobe

open to below

38'-0"

47'-11"

Nook
9/6x8/6

Family
13/0x16/0

Kit.

Dining
10/0x12/0
vaulted

Living
12/6x17/6
vaulted

Garage
19/0x20/6

w. d.

ref.

can.

f.

BARCLAY HOME DESIGNS

Soaring Entry Opens Family Plan

No. 90557

Towering columns create dramatic exterior impact, but the central entry of this elegant family home will take your breath away. Dominated by an

impressive staircase, this incredible space provides easy access to every room, from the vaulted living and dining rooms to informal areas at the rear of the house. If you like to cook, you'll love the sunny, island kitchen that opens to the family room. Dine informally in the adjoining nook, or have a barbecue on the patio. When you want to escape from the everyday

bustle, retreat to the den, or upstairs to the garden tub in your private master suite. Notice the built-in desks with streetside views in the front bedrooms.

First floor — 1,475 sq. ft.
Second floor — 1,060 sq. ft.
Garage — 2-car

Total living area — 2,535 sq. ft.

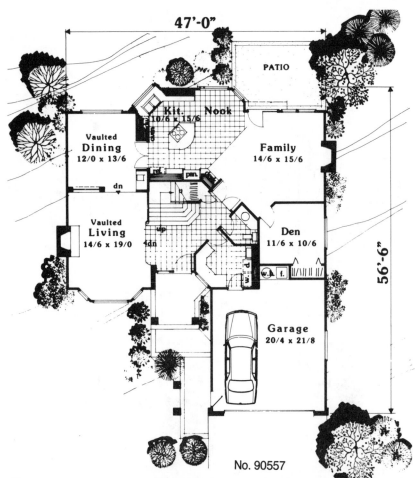

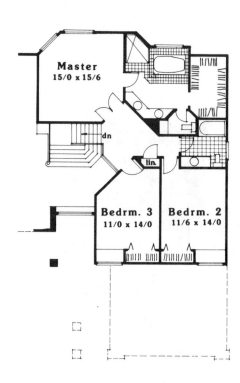

No. 90557

An Asset to Any Neighborhood

No. 90556

With abundant rear-facing windows, this clapboard classic takes full advantage of a beautiful backyard view. Interior views are just as exciting. From the angular staircase, you can look down over the fireplaced living and dining rooms, or glance up at the balcony hall that links four bedrooms and two full baths.   A desk in the back bedroom, twin vanities in the master bath, and a cozy window seat in the front bedroom add convenience and help cut clutter. You'll find the same efficient approach in active areas, with built-ins in the fireplaced family room, a pantry tucked under the stairs in the U-shaped kitchen, and the side-by-side arrangement of powder and laundry rooms just behind the garage.

First floor — 1,055 sq. ft.

Second floor — 1,030 sq. ft.

Garage — 2-car

Total living area — 2,085 sq. ft.

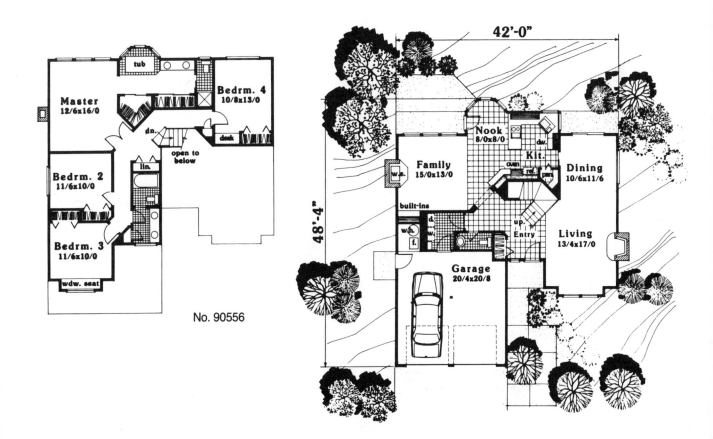

No. 90556

Spacious Living in a Small Package

No. 91401

Do you have a small lot and big dreams? Here's a perfect solution: a compact house with three bedrooms and a wonderful, wide-open feeling. Step into the vaulted living room, made even larger by a two-story arched window. At the rear of the house, the family room, sunny dining bay, and well-appointed kitchen with a huge pantry unite in one spacious area. This open plan allows heat from the energy-saving wood stove to circulate throughout the house. With a private deck and a luxurious bath with double vanities, a shower, and oversized tub, the master suite at the top of the stairs is a magnificent retreat you're sure to appreciate. Specify a crawlspace or basement when ordering this plan.

First floor — 924 sq. ft.
Second floor — 860 sq. ft.
Garage — 430 sq. ft.

Total living area — 1,784 sq. ft.

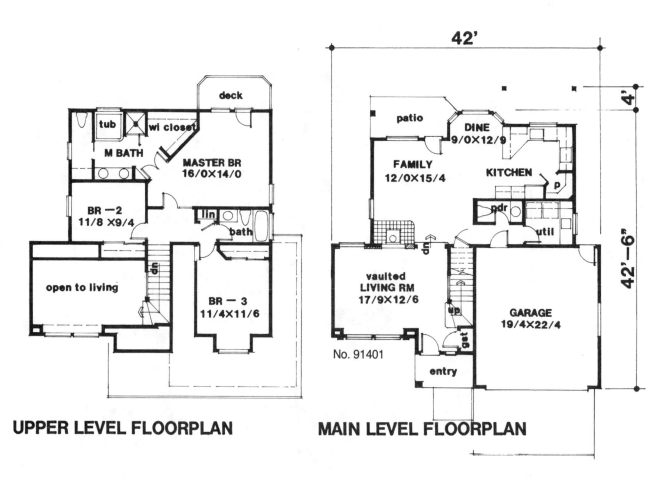

UPPER LEVEL FLOORPLAN

MAIN LEVEL FLOORPLAN

Arches Grace
Alluring Exterior

No. 99304

Soaring roof lines punctuated by arched gables and a towering chimney hint at the dramatic interior of this distinctive family home. Step down from the entry to an exciting, fireplaced living room that rises two stories. Two dining rooms flank the efficient L-shaped kitchen. The sunny breakfast room is just right for family meals. But, when you're entertaining, the formal dining room is an elegant spot for a special meal, with French doors to a rear deck adding a touch of romance to the festivities. Bedrooms, placed on the upper floor for privacy, feature walk-in closets. Two bedrooms are served by a full bath at the top of the stairs, but the vaulted master suite features its own bath with walk-in shower.

First floor — 686 sq. ft.
Second floor — 645 sq. ft.
Garage — 2-car

Total living area —1,331 sq. ft.

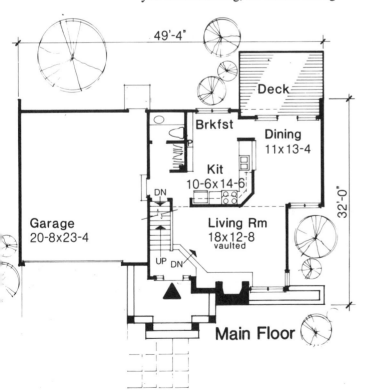

Main Floor

49'-4"

Deck

Brkfst

Dining
11x13-4

Kit
10-6x14-6

DN

Living Rm
18x12-8
vaulted

Garage
20-8x23-4

32'-0"

UP DN

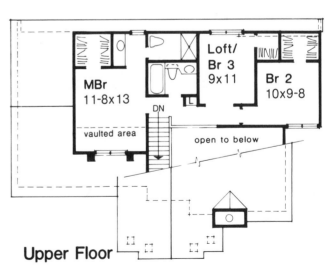

Upper Floor

MBr
11-8x13

vaulted area

Loft/
Br 3
9x11

Br 2
10x9-8

DN

open to below

No. 99304

Attractive and Affordable

No. 90387

Plants and people alike will love the sunny atmosphere of this cheerful, three-bedroom home. The raised entry, dominated by a stairway to the second floor, overlooks the sunken living room. Wrap-around windows and soaring ceilings add dramatic impact to this spacious area, warmed by the cozy glow of a fireplace. Look at the country kitchen at the rear of the house, with its greenhouse window, pass-through convenience to the formal dining room, and sliders to the rear deck. Upstairs, bedrooms are arranged for convenience. The full bath features two-way access: from the hallway, and through a private entrance in the master bedroom. Notice the beautiful alcove created by the half-round window in the front bedroom.

First floor — 713 sq. ft.
Second floor — 691 sq. ft.
Garage — 2-car

Total living area — 1,404 sq. ft.

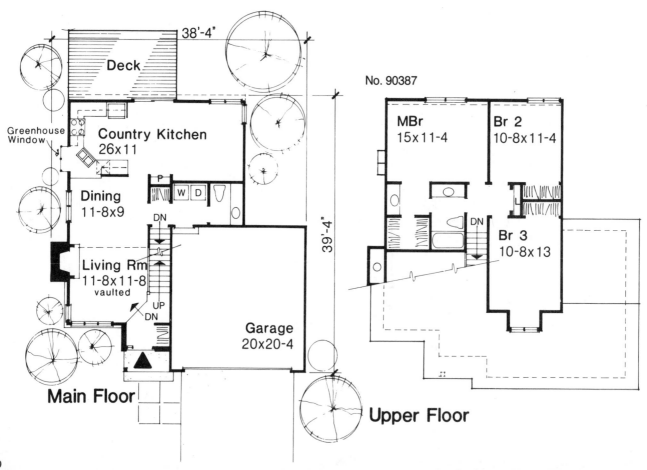

Small but Spacious

No. 91312

Remove unnecessary hallways and walls, add an abundant supply of windows, and you've got a compact contemporary with a wide-open feeling. Stand in the spacious entry, dominated by an open staircase. To the left, a fireplaced family room adjoins a bay-windowed breakfast nook off the kitchen. To the right, an elegant, sunken living room, featuring a corner window arrangement and cheerful bay, is steps away from the formal dining room. You'll love the compact kitchen at the rear of the house, convenient to both eating areas. Upstairs, the two front bedrooms share a spectacular, arched window and a double-vanitied full bath. The rear master suite enjoys a private bath and sunny bay sitting nook.

First floor — 879 sq. ft.
Second floor — 746 sq. ft.
Garage — 2-car

Total living area — 1,625 sq. ft.

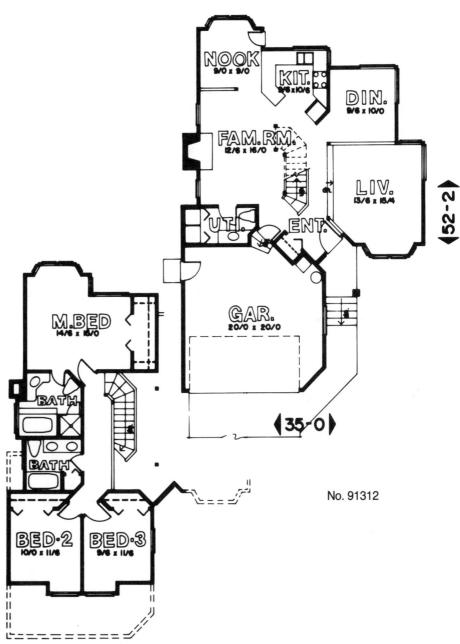

No. 91312

Four Bedroom 1-1/2 Story Design

No. 90358

Many of today's single family markets are looking for a flexible plan that grows and adapts to their family's changing needs. This is such a house with its master bedroom and den/4th bedroom down, double bedrooms up, stacked baths and well-working open and flowing living areas. The exterior impact is of hi-style, hi-value, the interior is highlighted by the vaulted living room and thru views to the rear deck and yard. This house belongs in a neighborhood where the custom exterior look will make for a surprising space-value combination to the move-up young family market.

Main floor — 1,062 sq. ft.
Upper floor — 469 sq. ft.
Garage — 2-car

Total living area — 1,531 sq. ft.

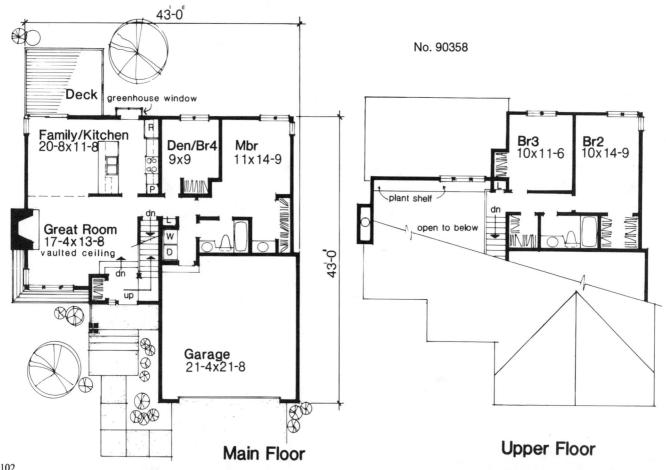

Main Floor

Upper Floor

Designed for an Informal Life Style

No. 90325

You'll find daily living relaxed and comfortable in this stylish plan. Both the Great room and the kitchen/dining room of this home are accented by vaulted ceilings. In addition to having a conveniently arranged L-shaped food preparation center, the dining area overlooks the deck through sliding glass doors. The Great room incorporates all adjacent floor space and is highlighted by the corner placement of the fireplace. Two bedrooms are secluded from the living areas and feature individual access to the full bath. The master bedroom also includes a separate vanity in the dressing area.

Main living area — 988 sq. ft.
Basement — 988 sq. ft.
Garage — 400 sq. ft.

Total living area — 988 sq. ft.

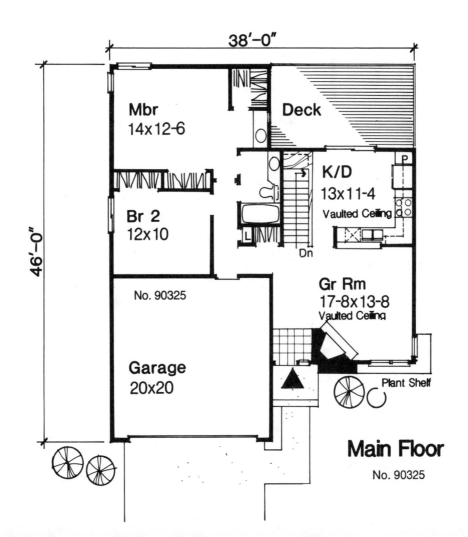

Main Floor

No. 90325

Arch Recalls Another Era

No. 90675

Massive roof lines pierced with clerestory windows only hint at the interior excitement of this contemporary beauty. The vaulted foyer of this elegant home, graced by Doric columns that support an elegant arch, lends an air of ancient Greece to the spacious living and dining rooms. To the right, a well-appointed peninsula kitchen features pass-over convenience to the adjoining dinette bay and family room. Open the sliding glass doors to add an outdoor feeling to every room at the rear of the house. The ample master suite features a private terrace and whirlpool bath. A hall bath serves the other bedrooms in the sleeping wing off the entry.

Main living area — 1,558 sq. ft.
Laundry/mudroom — 97 sq. ft.
Garage — 2-car

Total living area — 1,655 sq. ft.

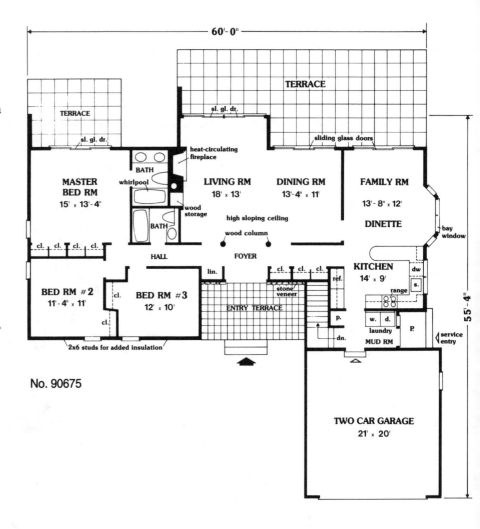

No. 90675

Low Budget Luxury

No. 90631

This contemporary house uses nature's energy and an architect's intelligence for economy with style. The family room/kitchen features a greenhouse sun space and access to a large deck made for relaxed entertaining. Clerestory windows and an attractive bay window bring sunlight and fresh air into the living room which features a prefabricated, heat-circulating fireplace. The master bedroom has its own bath with shower and two closets, one of them a walk-in. Two other bedrooms share a full bath. A laundry is off the attached garage. With this plan, you can save money without sacrificing the benefits of good design.

Main living area — 1,369 sq. ft.
Garage — 220 sq. ft.
Basement — 1,268 sq. ft.

Total living area — 1,589 sq. ft.

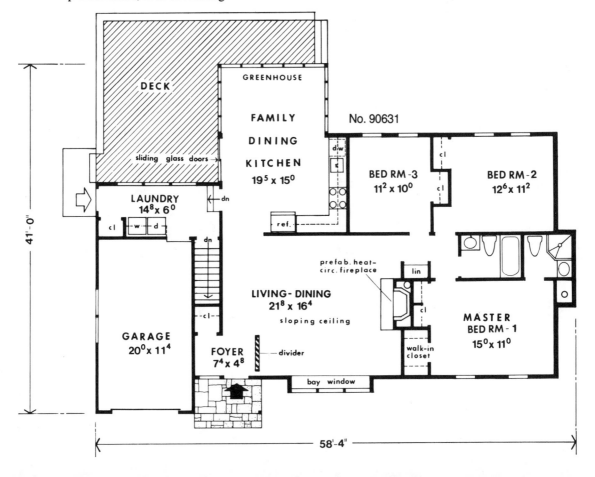

Appealing Contemporary Design

No. 90366

The story-and-a-half house provides an opportunity to combine old-fashioned value with contemporary design appeal. This house looks and lives contemporary with its dramatic entrance and vaulted ceiling space, its garden kitchen, its flexible, open living-dining-kitchen area and its generous master bedroom dressing closet. Note also, the modern convenience of the mudroom-laundry entrance. Yet, with a door to block hallway access, the upstairs can be left unfinished to reduce initial cash requirements. The two bedrooms and bath with an optional operable skylight can be a do-it-yourself project to be finished later. If built without a basement, mechanical equipment can be placed under the stairs.

Main living area — 1,549 sq. ft.

Total living area — 1,549 sq. ft.

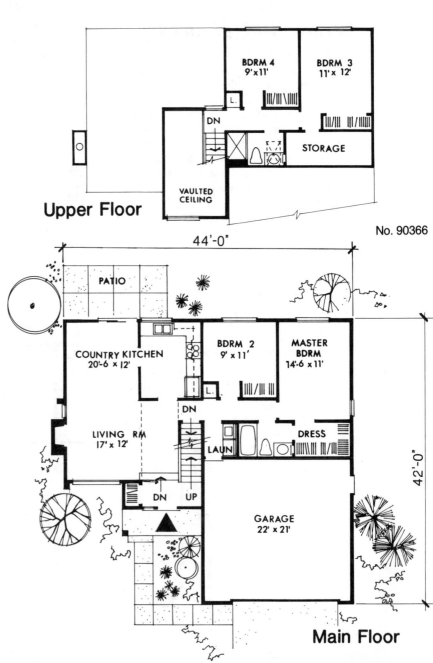

Upper Floor

BDRM 4
9' x 11'

BDRM 3
11' x 12'

DN

STORAGE

VAULTED CEILING

No. 90366

44'-0"

PATIO

COUNTRY KITCHEN
20'-6 x 12'

BDRM 2
9' x 11'

MASTER BDRM
14'-6 x 11'

DN

LIVING RM
17' x 12'

LAUN

DRESS

42'-0"

DN   UP

GARAGE
22' x 21'

Main Floor

Contemporary Offers Sunken Living Room

No. 90334

This contemporary design is inviting because of the built-in greenhouse that is located just left of the entry into the house. Inside, a sunken living room is accessible from the hallway. Once in the living room, you're greeted by a vaulted ceiling and a masonry fireplace. A formal dining room is located next to the living room. An efficient kitchen has a connecting breakfast room which appears larger because of its vaulted ceiling. An outside wooden deck is accessible from the kitchen-breakfast rooms. The family room has its own wood-burning fireplace and a wetbar. Laundry facilities are located near the family room. The second floor includes four bedrooms. The master bedroom has a his-hers walk-in closet, a whirlpool bath surrounded by tile and a cathedral ceiling with circle top windows.

First floor — 1,382 sq. ft.
Second floor — 1,328 sq. ft.

Total living area — 2,710 sq. ft.

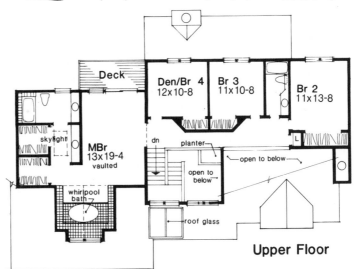

Upper Floor

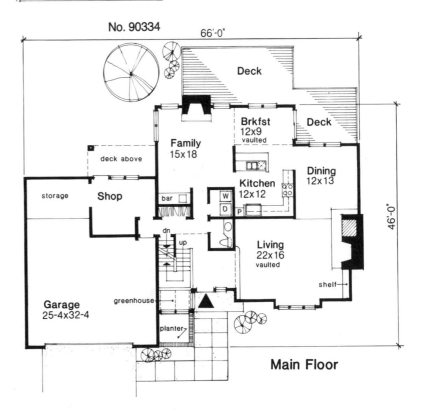

Main Floor

Soaring Ceilings, Multiple Levels Add Contemporary Flair

No. 90270

Do you have a lot with a great view? Here's a home with a wide-open feeling that will take advantage of that attractive location. Look at the windows and sliding glass doors linking every room with the great outdoors. The central entry divides the home into active and quiet areas. Three bedrooms and two full baths include the master suite with raised tub, step in shower, and private terrace entrance. Railings separate the massive gathering-dining room from the entry hall. And, when there's a chill in the air, the open arrangement allows every room to benefit from the warmth of the family room fireplace. The efficient island kitchen adjoining the informal eating nook completes a home your family will love.

Main living area — 2,652 sq. ft.
Garage — 2-car

Total living area — 2,652 sq. ft.

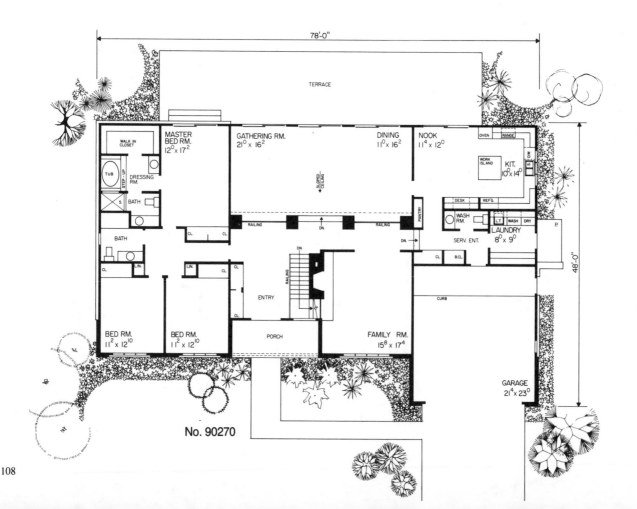

No. 90270

Welcoming Skylights Greet All

No. 99623

The impressive entrance foyer of this one-story contemporary features a high ceiling and six skylights. The living room has a partly trayed ceiling — its flat portion is 10 feet high. To the rear is a wood deck encompassing the entire back. A heat-circulating fireplace is enhanced with a decorative mantel surrounded by stone to the ceiling. The spacious formal dining room is adjacent to the combined kitchen, family room, and dinette featuring a greenhouse bay. The all-purpose room can be used as a library, den, or fourth bedroom. The master bedroom is equipped with a private deck and whirlpool tub.

Main living area — 1,789 sq. ft.
Laundry/mudroom — 119 sq. ft.
Garage and storage — 447 sq. ft.

Total living area — 1,789 sq. ft.

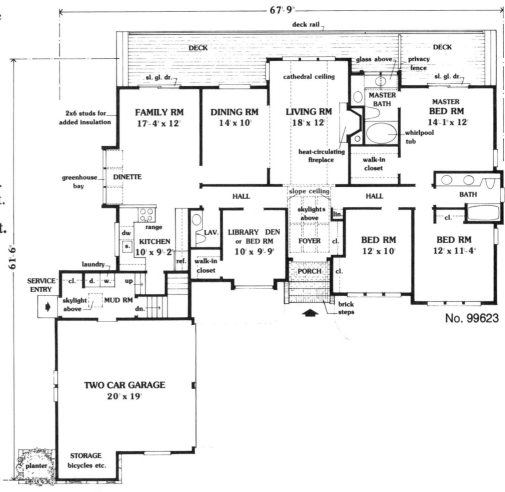

No. 99623

Glass Walls Brighten Second-Story Living

No. 90912

If you can't be outside on the sundecks, you can certainly enjoy your view from anywhere in this three-bedroom beauty. The protected portico enters an attractive foyer that leads to the family room, extra bedroom, and practical, full-sized utility space. Up the open staircase, the main floor is spacious and comfortable. You'll immediately notice the corner fireplace and soaring, vaulted ceiling of the sunken living room. The ample kitchen, with loads of counter space, is adjacent to family and dining rooms for convenient entertaining.

Main living area— 1,464 sq. ft.
Unfinished daylight basement — 1,183 sq. ft.
Garage — 422 sq. ft.
Width — 48'-0"
Depth — 39'-0"

Total living area —1,464 sq. ft.

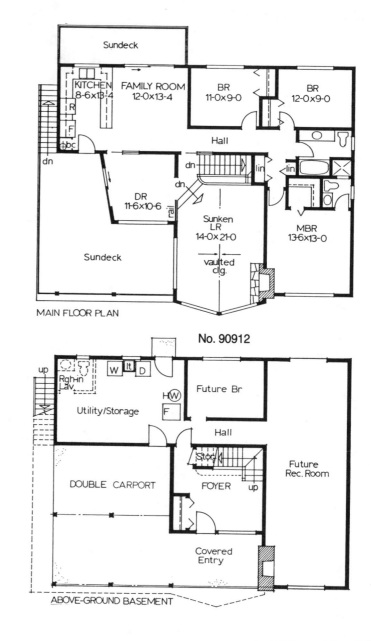

A Home for All Season

No. 90629

The natural cedar and stone exterior of this contemporary gem is virtually maintenance free, and its dramatic lines echo the excitement inside. There are so many luxurious touches in this plan: the two-story living room overlooked by an upper-level balcony, a massive stone wall that pierces the roof and holds two fireplaces, a kitchen oven and an outdoor barbecue. Outdoor dining is a pleasure with the barbecue so handy to the kitchen. All the rooms boast outdoor decks, and each bedroom has its own. The front entrance, garage, a dressing room with bath, and laundry room occupy the lower level.

Main level — 1,001 sq. ft.
Upper level — 712 sq. ft.
Lower level — 463 sq. ft.

Total living area — 2,176 sq. ft.

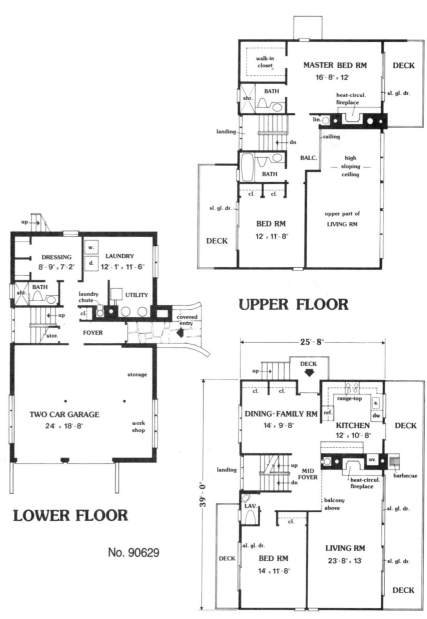

UPPER FLOOR

LOWER FLOOR

No. 90629

MAIN FLOOR

Skylit Bonus

No. 91632

With its graceful clapboard exterior, arched windows, and twin chimneys, this magnificent home recalls classic details of the past. But inside, you'll find all the amenities desired by today's family. The central foyer, flanked by a cozy den and formal living and dining room arrangement, is dominated by an L-shaped staircase. Step past the powder room, tucked under the stairs, to a sprawling, open space warmed by the family room fireplace. A rear deck completes informal areas, which include a well-appointed kitchen and sunny eating nook. Front-facing rooms upstairs are flooded with sun from the elegant arched windows that dominate them. Two full baths, one in the master suite, feature double vanities for early morning convenience.

First floor — 1,230 sq. ft.
Second floor — 952 sq. ft.
Bonus room — 295 sq. ft.
Garage — 2-car

Total living area — 2,182 sq. ft.

No. 91632

UPPER FLOOR

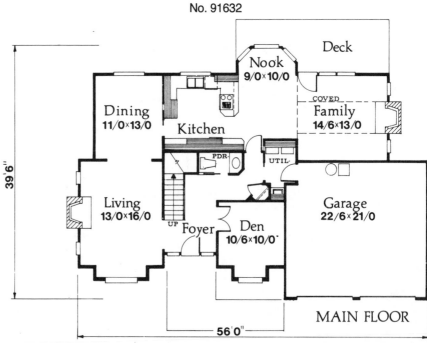

MAIN FLOOR

Kitchen Has Gourmet in Mind

No. 91429

The exterior of this home has contemporary lines with traditional overtones and wood shake accents. It utilizes the Great room design concept with an emphasis on gourmet-type kitchen planning. The "swing-back" staircase connects to the balcony overlooking the Great room. The gallery hall, which accesses the powder room, guest bedroom and den, is a perfect place for those family portraits. The second floor houses the master bedroom suite, which features a private deck, walk-in closet, comparmentalized bath, and another bedroom with its own bathroom. Basement plan is available, please specify when ordering.

First floor — 1,392 sq. ft.
Second floor — 832 sq. ft.
Garage — 2-car

Total living area — 2,224 sq. ft.

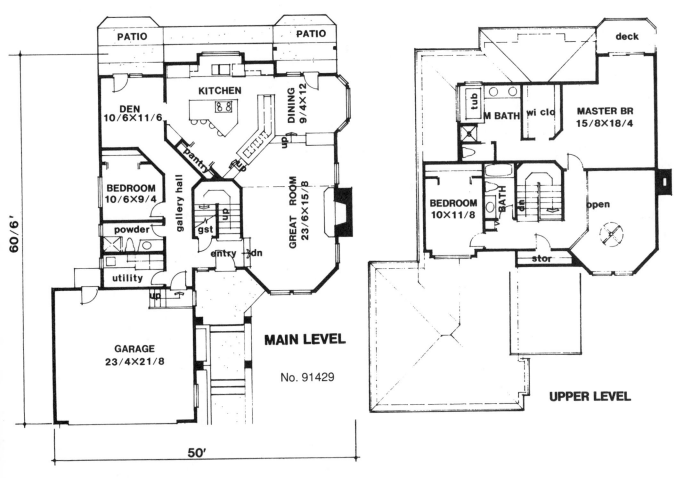

Friendly Facade

No. 20175

Day or night, this brick-accented beauty will present a friendly face to guests and passers-by. Abundant windows brighten every room, combining with an open plan to create a spacious charm that's hard to equal. Columns separate the living and dining rooms, so that the soaring ceilings and fireplace in the living room are enjoyed in both rooms. And their proximity to the kitchen and adjoining breakfast room makes entertaining easy. You'll love the convenience and the privacy of a first-floor master suite with skylit luxury bath. And the kids will appreciate the huge closets in the three bedrooms upstairs, as well as the view of the foyer and living room from the balcony that links their rooms with the hall bath.

First floor — 1,800 sq. ft.
Second floor — 790 sq. ft.
Basement — 1,800 sq. ft.
Garage — 559 sq. ft.

Total living area — 2,590 sq. ft.

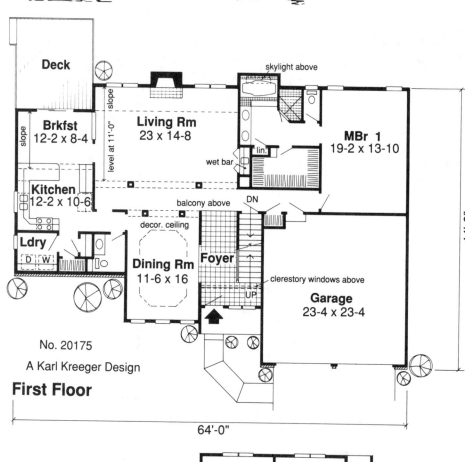

Deck

Brkfst
12-2 x 8-4

Living Rm
23 x 14-8

skylight above

MBr 1
19-2 x 13-10

wet bar

lin.

Kitchen
12-2 x 10-6

balcony above

DN

decor. ceiling

Ldry

D W

Dining Rm
11-6 x 16

Foyer

UP

clerestory windows above

Garage
23-4 x 23-4

No. 20175

A Karl Kreeger Design

First Floor

64'-0"

44'-0"

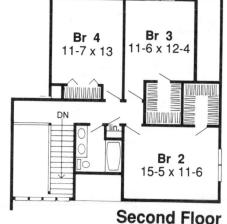

Br 4
11-7 x 13

Br 3
11-6 x 12-4

DN

lin.

Br 2
15-5 x 11-6

Second Floor

First-Time Owner's Delight

No. 20063

A distinctive exterior of wood veneer siding with a large, picture window combines with just a touch of brick to set this simple one-and-a-half story design into a class of its own. On the first level, the foyer leads directly into the living room which has a fireplace and is open to the dining room. The kitchen lies just to the left of the dining room. A laundry room is conveniently placed between the kitchen and the garage. The master bedroom lies on the first floor and has a full bath and walk-in closet. On the second floor two more bedrooms exist and share a full bath. There is also a loft area open to the living room below.

First floor — 1,161 sq. ft.
Second floor — 631 sq. ft.
Garage — 2-car

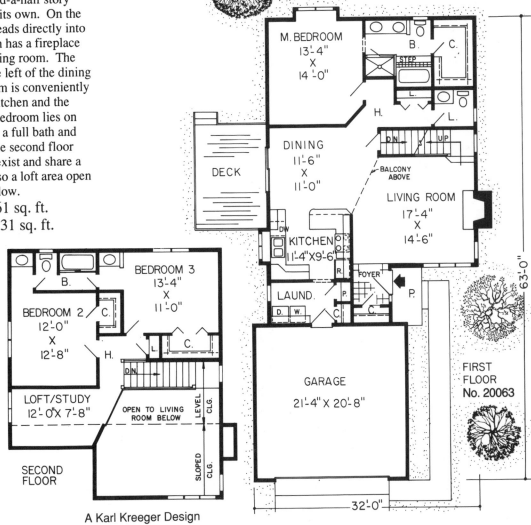

Total living area — 1,792 sq. ft.

M. BEDROOM
13'-4" X 14'-0"
B.
C.
STEP
L.
H.
L.
DECK
DINING
11'-6" X 11'-0"
DN
UP
BALCONY ABOVE
LIVING ROOM
17'-4" X 14'-6"
DW
KITCHEN
11'-4" X 9'-6"
R.
FOYER
LAUND.
D. W.
C.
P.
P.
GARAGE
21'-4" X 20'-8"
63'-0"
FIRST FLOOR
No. 20063
32'-0"

BEDROOM 3
13'-4" X 11'-0"
B.
BEDROOM 2
12'-0" X 12'-8"
C.
H.
L.
C.
DN
LOFT/STUDY
12'-0" X 7'-8"
OPEN TO LIVING ROOM BELOW
LEVEL
CLG.
SLOPED CLG.
CLG.
SECOND FLOOR

A Karl Kreeger Design

Enjoy the View

No. 90833

Here's a house that will take advantage
of your location to create an irresistible
view from the second floor. On the
lower level, you'll find a bayed family
room complete with a fireplace just off
the foyer. But, the main living areas
are upstairs. The L-shaped staircase
brings you right into the living room.
Bay windows, the open railing, and
adjacent dining area with sliding glass
doors to the sundeck give this area a
spacious feeling. The family kitchen is
large enough to accommodate a table
for informal meals. Past the pantry and
full bath, three bedrooms occupy the
rear of the house, away from active
areas and the noise of the street.

Basement floor — 994 sq. ft.
Main floor — 1,318 sq. ft.
Garage — 378 sq. ft.
Width — 40 ft.
Depth — 40 ft.

Total living area — 1,318 sq. ft.

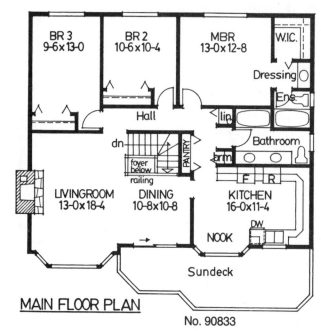

MAIN FLOOR PLAN

No. 90833

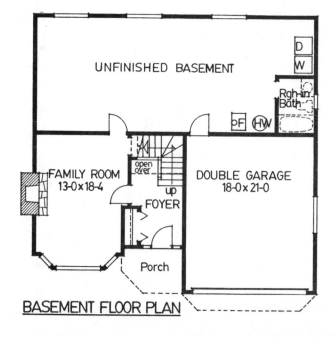

BASEMENT FLOOR PLAN

Contemporary Height

No. 10675

Vertical siding and stacked windows combine to create a soaring facade for this three-bedroom contemporary. Inside, sloping ceilings, bump out windows, and an open staircase unite the foyer, living room and formal dining room into one bright, airy space. The fireplaced family room and breakfast nook flanking the kitchen both open to an outdoor deck at the rear of the house. You'll find a full bath that serves two ample bedrooms right at the top of the stairs. And to the right, behind double doors, lies a luxurious master suite with skylit bath, walk-in closet, and double vanities.

First floor — 969 sq. ft.
Second floor — 714 sq. ft.
Basement — 969 sq. ft.
Garage — 484 sq. ft.

Total living area — 1,683 sq. ft.

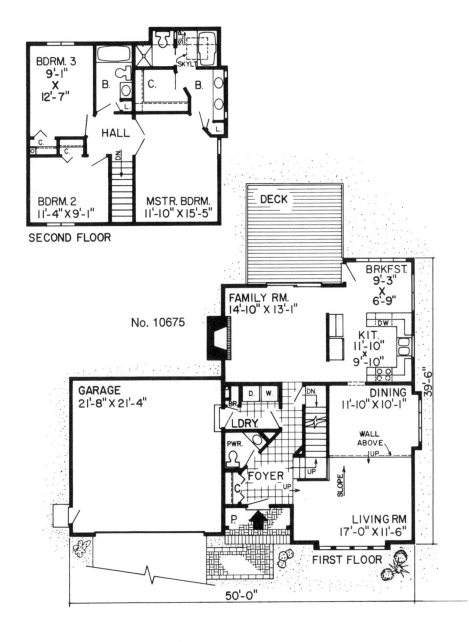

Build this House in a Beautiful Spot

No. 90672

This family home combines the charm of an early American Saltbox with contemporary drama. With a rear wall that's almost entirely glass and soaring ceilings pierced by skylights, active areas on the first floor unite with a full-length deck and back yard for an incredible outdoor feeling. But, beauty doesn't mean convenience has to be compromised. Look at the efficient galley kitchen, the adjoining pantry right by the rear entry, and the first-floor master bedroom served by a full bath. Survey the living areas below from the second floor balcony that opens to two bedrooms and another full bath.

First floor — 1,042 sq. ft.
Second floor — 519 sq. ft.
Mud/laundry room — 58 sq. ft.
Basement — 1,000 sq. ft.
Garage — 234 sq. ft.

Total living area — 1,619 sq. ft.

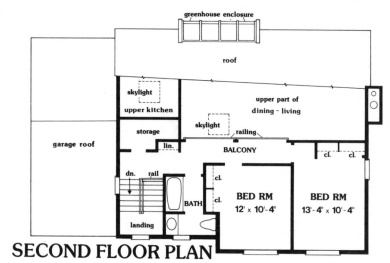

SECOND FLOOR PLAN

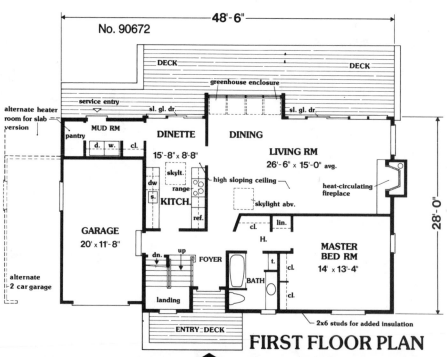

FIRST FLOOR PLAN

Three Fireplaces Will Keep You Warm

No. 91030

Have you always wanted your own private getaway, where you could just kick off your shoes and relax? You'll find it in the luxurious master suite in this distinctive four-bedroom home. The built-in spa is a feature you'll welcome at the end of your day. And the fireplace, glass blocks, and skylights make this a sunny, warm retreat. On the main level, bay windows brighten the living room and nook. The kitchen, which features a cooktop island, is centrally located for convenient meal service to formal and informal dining rooms.

First floor — 1,207 sq. ft.
Second floor — 1,341 sq. ft.

Total living area — 2,548 sq. ft.

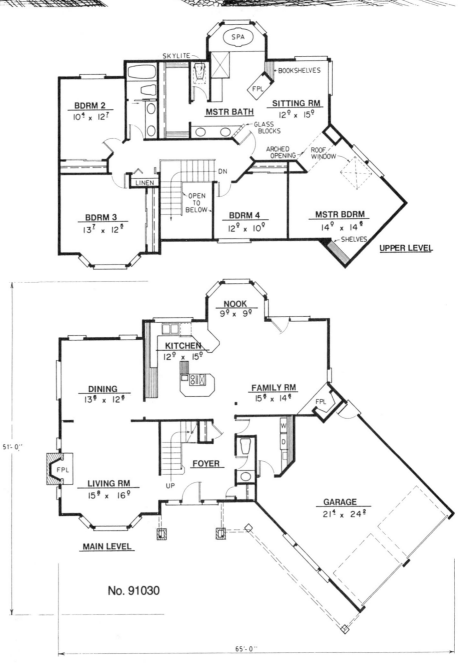

SPA

SKYLITE

BOOKSHELVES

BDRM 2
10⁴ x 12⁷

MSTR BATH

SITTING RM
12⁹ x 15⁹

FPL

GLASS BLOCKS

ARCHED OPENING

ROOF WINDOW

LINEN

DN

OPEN TO BELOW

BDRM 3
13⁷ x 12⁹

BDRM 4
12⁹ x 10⁹

MSTR BDRM
14⁹ x 14⁸

SHELVES

UPPER LEVEL

NOOK
9⁹ x 9⁹

KITCHEN
12⁹ x 15⁹

DINING
13⁹ x 12⁹

FAMILY RM
15⁹ x 14⁹

FPL

W
D

FPL

LIVING RM
15⁹ x 16⁹

FOYER

UP

GARAGE
21⁴ x 24²

51'-0"

MAIN LEVEL

No. 91030

65'-0"

Special Features Enhance Plan

No. 90365

The central entrance gives immediate impact indoors with a two-story, open stairwell. The living room also has a vaulted ceiling up to the stair landing overlook. A generous family room is stepped down for another change of spatial character. A garden kitchen and breakfast area extend indoor space to the deck outside, as does the greenhouse window box in the dining room. Convenience and luxury features are highlighted. Note the pantry, broom closet, microwave oven, trash compactor, five-foot wetbar and first-floor laundry-mud room. Upstairs note the optional fourth bedroom or master suite retreat, the attic for extra storage, the oversized master bathing pool-tub and the large master closet.

First floor — 1,310 sq. ft.
Second floor — 1,104 sq. ft.

Total living area — 2,414 sq. ft.

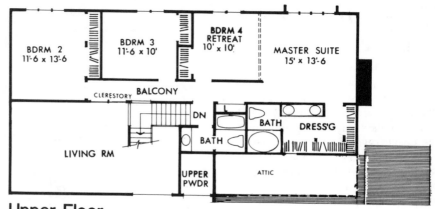

Upper Floor

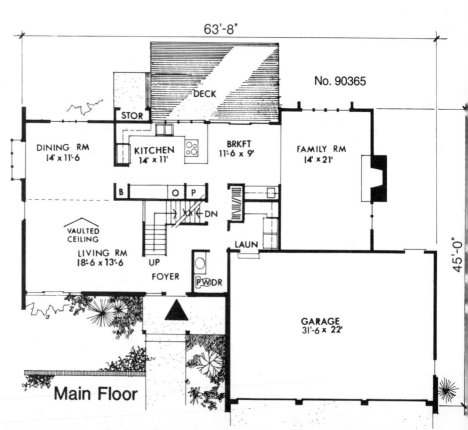

Main Floor

Easy Access; Easy Living

No. 99338

The living and dining rooms access a large deck, inviting outdoor meals and entertaining. The massive fireplace is flanked on each side by windows creating spectacular landscape views. A columned arcade divides living and dining areas. The bedroom off the front entrance might serve well as a den or office. The vaulted master suite includes walk-in wardrobe, luxurious spa bathing, and access to the deck.

Main living area — 1,642 sq. ft.

Basement — 1,642 sq. ft.

Garage — 2-car

Total living area — 1,642 sq. ft.

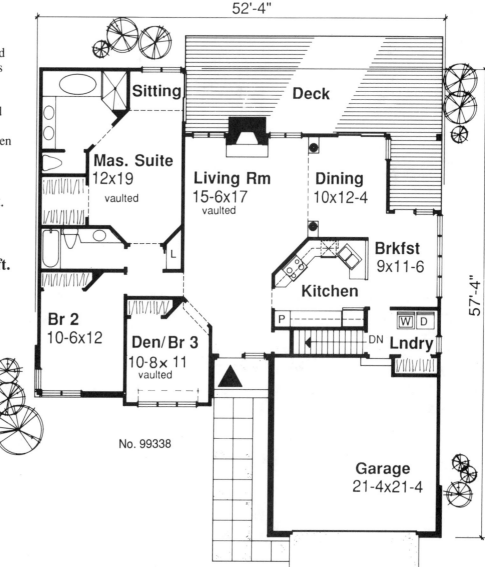

52'-4"

Sitting

Deck

Mas. Suite
12x19
vaulted

Living Rm
15-6x17
vaulted

Dining
10x12-4

Brkfst
9x11-6

Kitchen

Br 2
10-6x12

Den/ Br 3
10-8x 11
vaulted

P

W D

DN

Lndry

No. 99338

Garage
21-4x21-4

57'-4"

Contemporary Traditions

No. 99339

Traditional elements such as half-round and divided sash, covered front porch, gable louver detail and wrap-around plant shelf under corner windows all create a nostalgic appeal. Dramatic views await guests from the front entry, with a vaulted ceiling above the living room and clerestory glass, fireplace corner windows with half-round transom, and a long view through the dining room slider to the rear deck. The main floor master suite has corner windows, walk-in wardrobe and private bath access.

Main floor — 857 sq. ft.
Upper floor — 446 sq. ft.
Garage — 2-car

Total living area — 1,303 sq. ft.

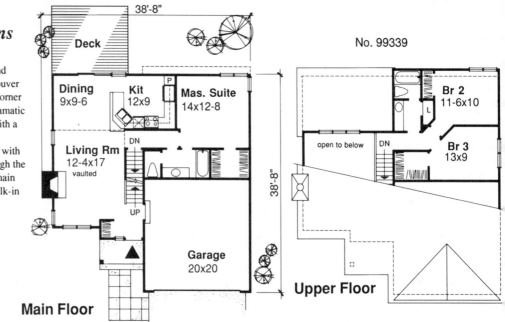

No. 99339

38'-8"

Deck

Dining 9x9-6

Kit 12x9

P

Mas. Suite 14x12-8

Living Rm 12-4x17 vaulted

DN

UP

38'-8"

Garage 20x20

Main Floor

Upper Floor

open to below

DN

Br 2 11-6x10

L

Br 3 13x9

Interior and Exterior Unity Distinguishes Plan

No. 90398

Are you a sun worshipper? A rear orientation and a huge, wrap-around deck make this one-level home an outdoor lover's dream. Stepping into the entry, you're afforded a panoramic view of active areas, from the exciting vaulted living room to the angular kitchen overlooking the cheerful breakfast nook. Columns divide the living and dining rooms. Half-walls separate the kitchen and breakfast room. And, the result is a sunny celebration of open space not often found in a one-level home. Bedrooms feature special window treatments and interesting angles. A full bath serves the two front bedrooms, but the luxurious master suite boasts its own private, skylit bath with double vanities, as well as a generous walk-in closet.

Main living area — 1,630 sq. ft.
Garage — 2-car

Total living area — 1,630 sq. ft.

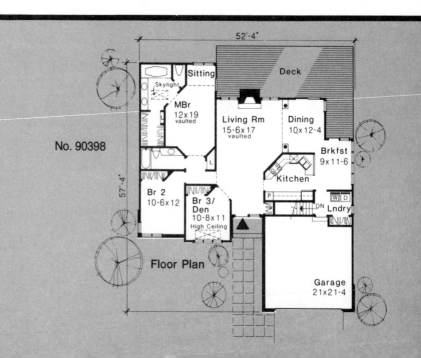

No. 90398

52'-4"

57'-4"

Sitting
Skylight

MBr 12x19 vaulted

L

Br 2 10-6x12

Br 3/ Den 10-8x11
High Ceiling

Deck

Living Rm 15-6x17 vaulted

Dining 10x12-4

Brkfst 9x11-6

Kitchen

P

W D

DN

Lndry

Garage 21x21-4

Floor Plan

Plant Shelf Divides Living Space with Greenery

No. 90394

Twin gables, a beautiful half-round window, and Colonial-style corner boards give this one-story classic an inviting, traditional exterior that says "Welcome". Inside, the ingenious, open plan of active areas makes every room seem even larger. Look at the vaulted living room, where floor-to-ceiling windows provide a pleasing unity with the yard. In the spectacular dining room, which adjoins the kitchen for convenient mealtimes, sliding glass doors open to a rear deck. Three bedrooms at the rear of the house include the angular master suite, which features a private bath and double-sized closet.

Main living area — 1,252 sq. ft.
Garage — 2-car

Total living area — 1,252 sq. ft.

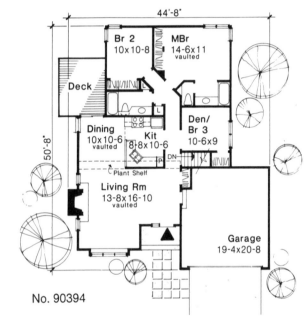

44'-8"

50'-8"

Br 2
10x10-8

MBr
14-6x11
vaulted

Deck

Dining
10x10-6
vaulted

Kit
8-8x10-6

Den/
Br 3
10-6x9

Plant Shelf

Living Rm
13-8x16-10
vaulted

Garage
19-4x20-8

No. 90394

Open Spaces

No. 91803

An attractive exterior encloses this exciting floor plan. There is a two-story ceiling in the foyer. The living room incorporates a 10 foot ceiling and transom windows. The kitchen features a large pantry and eating bar. The nook is adjacent to the main floor family room creating a very open feeling. Multi-level plant ledges highlight the U-shaped stairway, upstairs, the vaulted master suite has a private sitting area, and a dressing room with a walk-in closet, spa tub, and double sinks. The toilet and shower are located in a separate room insuring privacy. An open loft overlooks the foyer and stairway, two additional bedrooms and a fullbath complete the upper floor. Please specify basement, slab or crawlspace foundation when ordering.

Main floor — 1,129 sq. ft.
Second floor — 1,156 sq. ft.
Garage — 2-car

Total living area — 2,285 sq. ft.

No. 91803

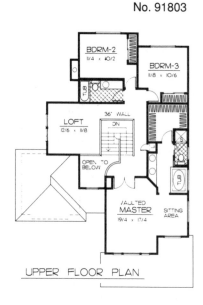

UPPER FLOOR PLAN

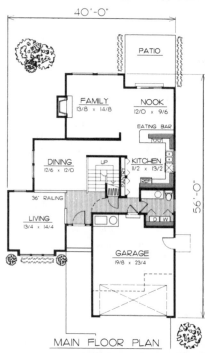

MAIN FLOOR PLAN

Master Retreat Crowns Contemporary Plan

No. 10625

The dramatic roof lines of this three-bedroom gem only hint at the wonderful angles that lie inside. From a sheltered porch, the foyer leads to a two-story great room with sloping ceilings and a huge fireplace. For outdoor lovers, the open plan unites the kitchen, dining, and living areas with a rear deck. Upstairs, dramatic angles are repeated in the master suite, tucked away, on its own landing, from other parts of the house. A few steps up, two more bedrooms share the upper reaches of this intriguing contemporary.

First floor — 990 sq. ft.
Second floor — 980 sq. ft.
Garage — 450 sq. ft.

Total living area —1,970 sq. ft.

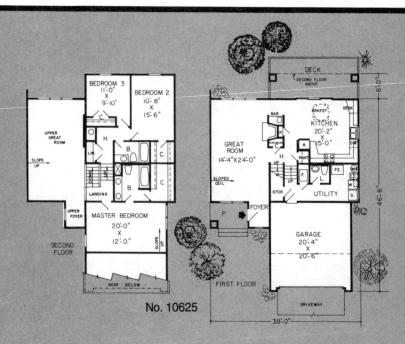

No. 10625

Angular Design is Strikingly Contemporary

No. 10469

The living room is the focal point of this contemporary design and incorporates several innovative features. Its vaulted-ceiling is highlighted with exposed beams, and the angled front has up to four levels of windows which are operated by remote control. A wood-burning fireplace and built-in bookshelves enhance the rear wall of the room. The kitchen, informal serving area and dining room occupy the remainder of the first floor. The second floor is reserved for the three spacious bedrooms. The master bedroom also has a beamed-ceiling plus its own fireplace.

First floor — 989 sq. ft.
Second floor — 810 sq. ft.
Garage — 538 sq. ft.

Total living area — 1,799 sq. ft.

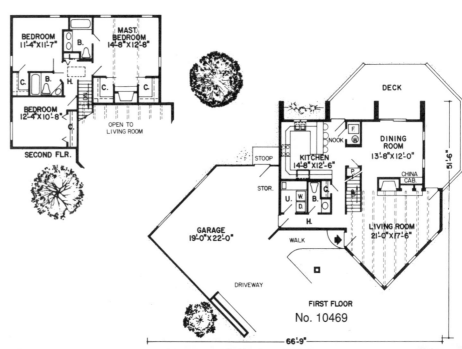

SECOND FLR.

BEDROOM 11'-4"x11'-7"

MAST. BEDROOM 14'-8"x12'-8"

BEDROOM 12'-4"x10'-8"

OPEN TO LIVING ROOM

DECK

KITCHEN 14'-8"x12'-6"

NOOK

DINING ROOM 13'-8"x12'-0"

CHINA CAB.

GARAGE 19'-0"x22'-0"

STOOP

STOR.

WALK

LIVING ROOM 21'-0"x17'-6"

DRIVEWAY

FIRST FLOOR
No. 10469

51'-6"

66'-9"

For Family Living

No. 91786

Atop this two-story home, a fireplace-equipped master suite and other bedrooms stand ready to revitalize a spent family with a good night's sleep. Below this private area, the main floor yields to both formal entertaining and less-formal pursuits. Built for a family, this three car-garage, low slung looker combines luxury and livability on a city lot. Visitors step down into a sunlit-dappled living room graced with vaulted ceilings. After cocktails, amble next door to the dining room, which opens onto the deck. The kitchen combines a country view with big-city sophistication. An island boasting a second "vegetable sink" and a full pantry are only some of its features. The nook acts as an in-house hideaway. The family room, of course, is a place for interaction. The master suite features a sitting room for those pensive moods and a walk-in closet for those fashion moods. Throw in a double-sink vanity and a huge shower and you have luxury.

Main floor — 1,532 sq. ft.
Second floor — 1,120 sq. ft.
Garage — 660 sq. ft.

Total living area — 2,652 sq. ft.

SECOND FLOOR PLAN

No. 91786

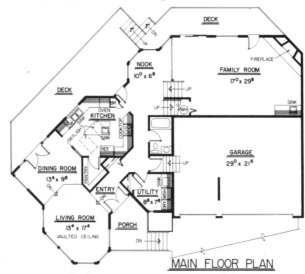

MAIN FLOOR PLAN

Semi-Circular Shaped Home

No. 91735

Brick columns and a brick facade give an air of humble but solid elegance to this home. A circular driveway sweeping past the front of this semi-circular shaped home completes the image. Family activities take place in the central section, which is comprised of an expansive array of rooms as large as many small homes. The large kitchen has a unique pantry. The eating nook is bright and cheerful, awash in natural light from the bay window. A woodstove warms both the nook and a family room. The living room, dining room and office are all located on the front-facing side of the group living area. The master suite has a huge walk-in closet. A pocket door separates the bathroom from the double vanities in the dressing area. Three additional bedrooms share a compartmentalized bathroom.

Main living area — 3,173 sq. ft.
Garage — 636 sq. ft.

No. 91735

FLOOR PLAN

Total living area — 3,173 sq. ft.

For Compact City Lot

No. 91783

By working with angles, the designer has created an attractive side yard that allows full utilization of an area that usually lies idle. While the garage sits squarely on the lot, far enough back from the street to meet set-back requirements, the living room is placed at an angle and is much closer to the street. The living room has a fireplace and wide bay windows. A wide deck wraps around the side and back of the home. It is accessible through sliding glass doors in the living room, dining room and kitchen. The country kitchen has a work island/eating bar combination, both a broom closet and a pantry, adding to the already generous couner and cupboard space. The master suite is set at an angle. It has a large walk-in closet and a spa tub. The other two bedrooms, one with a dormer window, share a bathroom.

Main floor — 967 sq. ft.
Second floor — 770 sq. ft.
Garage — 571 sq. ft.

Total living area — 1,737 sq. ft.

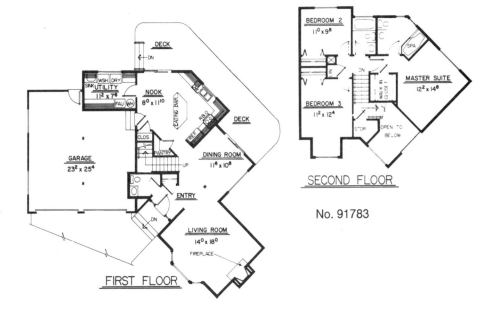

Economical Elegance

No. 91675

This plan has it all — Both formal and informal dining, a spacious kitchen with island, that directs you to a vaulted family room. A back stairway from the fireplaced family room leads you upstairs to a healthy second floor where not only do you have bonus space for the kids, but gives you space from the kids. The modern master bedroom features a coved ceiling and large master bath with a walk-in closet. Downstairs the living room features a fireplace and flows easily into the dining room for easy entertaining. Comtemporary elegance, yet economical, this plan says it all.

First floor — 1,370 sq. ft.
Second floor — 998 sq. ft.
Bonus — 321 sq. ft.
Garage — 756 sq. ft.

Total living area — 2,689 sq. ft.

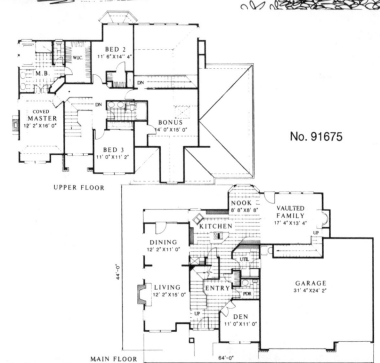

No. 91675

Spiral Stairs Lead to Loft

No. 90127

The central A-frame of this unusual design comprises the core of this home's living areas. The large eat-in kitchen easily serves the formal dining room or the Great room, which is accented by a cathedral ceiling, fireplace and sliding doors leading to the patio. Three bedrooms and a four-piece bath are gathered on one wing of the home while the master bedroom is further separated from the living areas by the placement of the laundry and the foyer. The master bath features individual dressing areas with a central bathing area. This arrangement is ideal for a working couple with teenagers.

First floor — 2,093 sq. ft.
Loft area — 326 sq. ft.

Total living area — 2,419 sq. ft.

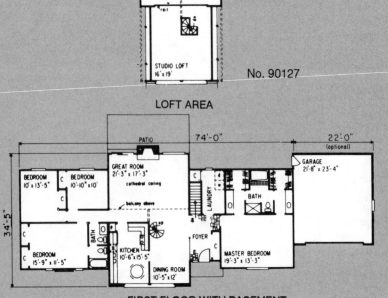

No. 90127

LOFT AREA

FIRST FLOOR WITH BASEMENT

Open Concept Plan

No.91430

This luxurious contemporary "open concept" plan was designed for the established family or couples who enjoy entertaining. The centrally located fireplace is the home's focal point offering visual privacy to the first floor areas. The breakfast room, kitchen and dining room have standard ceilings which emphasize the vaulted great room with its overhead balcony and its sweeping view of the backyard. Upstairs are two bedrooms which share a full bath, a library which overlooks the great room and the master bedroom suite with its private deck, double-vanitied bath and walk-in closet. A daylight basement version is available, please specify when ordering.

First floor — 2,030 sq. ft.
Second floor — 1,409 sq. ft.
Garage — 3-car

Total living area — 3,425 sq. ft.

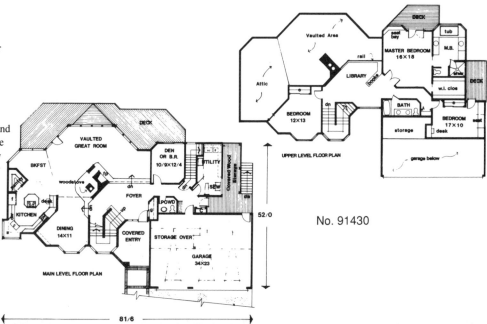

No. 91430

Compact Home for a Small Space

No. 90500

A massive bay window is the dominant feature in the facade of this cozy home with attached two-car garage. From the entry, there are three ways to walk. Turn left into the fireplaced living room and adjoining dining room. Or walk straight into the kitchen and breakfast nook, which extends to a covered porch. Step down the hall on the right to the master suite, full bath, and a second bedroom. The TV room, which can double as a third bedroom, completes the circular floor plan in this convenient, one-level abode.

Main living area — 1,299 sq. ft.
Garage—2-car

Total living area — 1,299 sq. ft.

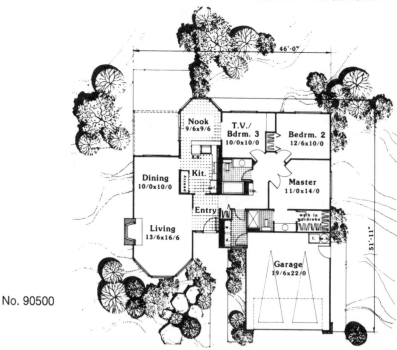

No. 90500

Traditional Transom Windows Add Appeal

No. 90396

Here's a compact charmer conceived with convenience in mind. The view from the entry is stunning. See the open staircase, the towering ceilings of the expansive, vaulted living and dining rooms, and the patio just outside in one, sweeping glance. Step beyond the staircase, and discover the garden atmosphere of a well-appointed, skylit kitchen. And, the first-floor master suite, with its dramatic vaulted ceilings, private patio access, and double-vanitied bath, couldn't be closer to the morning coffee. Two bedrooms and a full bath open to the second-floor balcony landing with a view of active areas.

First floor — 1,099 sq. ft.
Second floor — 452 sq. ft.
Garage — 2-car

Total living area — 1,551 sq. ft.

Main Floor

38'-4"

Master Suite
12-6x15-4
vaulted

Patio

Dining
12-4x10
vaulted

Kitchen
12-4x13

Living Rm
12-4x13-6
vaulted

Lndry

Garage
19-4x21-4

58'-0"

Upper Floor

Br 2
11-4x11

open to
below

Skylight

Br 3
11-4x10

No. 90396

Glass Walls Seem to Enlarge Front Living Areas

No. 10482

The second floor of this original design contains two bedrooms plus a shared walk-through path. Fronting the second floor are the stairway and a balcony which overlooks the glass-walled living room. The dining room also boasts a front glass wall and opens onto the efficient U-shaped kitchen. The full bath on the first floor may be accessed privately through the master bedroom or off the central hall. The laundry room, which also includes the utility area, is conveniently located between the kitchen and the master bedroom.

First floor — 966 sq. ft.
Second floor — 455 sq. ft.
Garage — 353 sq. ft.

Total living area — 1,421 sq. ft.

A Karl Kreeger Design
No. 10482

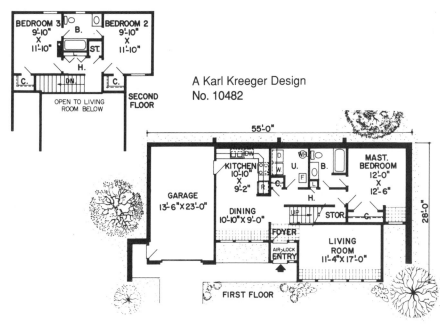

Beautiful Passive Solar Design

No. 90352

This dramatic, contemporary home is loaded with desirable features, as well as impressive passive solar benefits. The south-facing rear wall unites the vaulted Great room with the patio for an outdoor feeling. Glass-covered trombe walls and a greenhouse off the dining room capture the sun's warmth, combining with the fireplace to circulate warm air throughout the house. For even greater energy savings, berm along eastern and western exposures. Designed to keep the cook involved in the family action, the efficient, U-shaped kitchen features a convenient wetbar pass-through to the Great room. Three bedrooms, tucked in a private wing off the air-lock vestibule, include the spacious master suite with a skylit dressing area and private bath.
First floor — 1,418 sq. ft.

Total living area —1,418 sq. ft.

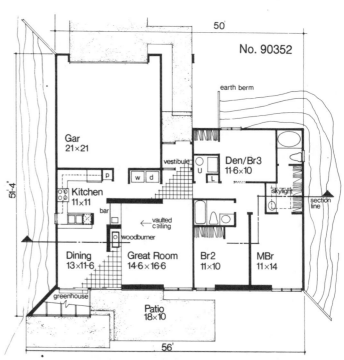

Open Loft Adds Charm To Passive Solar Design

No. 10542

The second floor loft, bounded on one side by a decorative railing, lends view to the spacious living room below. This four-bedroom beauty boasts all the comforts of home, including a jacuzzi in the master bedroom bath and a study just down the hall. For those who enjoy lots of views, a window seat spans the width of the living room windows. The large patio, located conveniently close to the kitchen, is ideal for those family get-togethers or for entertaining guests.
Main floor — 1,106 sq. ft.
Lower level (finished) — 746 sq. ft.
Lower level (unfinished) — 296 sq. ft.
Upper floor — 772 sq. ft.
Garage — 645 sq. ft.

Total living area —2,524 sq. ft.

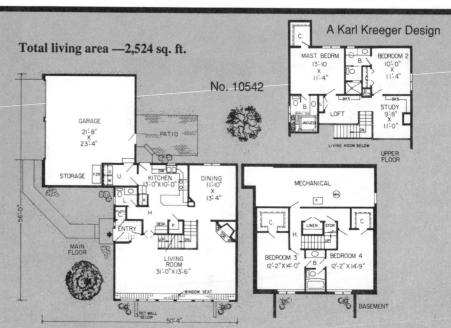

Solar Room More Than Just a Greenhouse

No. 90611

Thanks to the year-round solar room, this passive home will save you a bundle on your heating bills. Open the sliding glass doors on sunny days and close them at night to hold the heat inside the two-story living/dining room. A wrap-around deck adds warm weather living space. Two roomy bedrooms and a full bath complete the first floor. The master suite enjoys lofty views of the living area below. With a balcony, bath, and private sitting room, it's a pleasant retreat at the end of the day.

First floor — 1,120 sq. ft.
Second floor — 490 sq. ft.
Utility Room — 122 sq. ft.
(excluding solar room and deck)

Total living area —1,610 sq. ft.

SECOND FLOOR

No. 90611

FIRST FLOOR

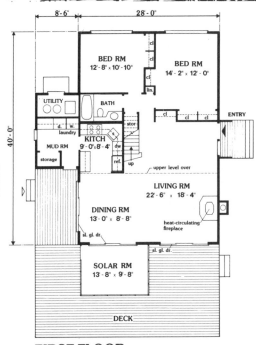

Contemporary Exterior

No. 90327

A spacious feeling is created by the ingenious arrangement of the living areas of this comfortable home. The inviting living room offers a cozy fireplace, a front corner full of windows, a vaulted ceiling and an open staircase. The clerestory windows further accent the open design of the dining room and kitchen. The U-shaped kitchen welcomes the cook and tasters alike with its open preparation areas. Secluded from the rest of the main floor and the other two bedrooms, the master bedroom features a walk-in closet and a large, compartmented bath which may also serve as a guest bathroom. Two additional bedrooms and a full bath comprise the upper floor.

Main floor — 846 sq. ft.
Upper floor — 400 sq. ft.
Basement — 846 sq. ft.
Garage — 400 sq. ft.

Total living area — 1,246 sq. ft.

No. 90327

Upper Floor

Main Floor

High Impact Angles

No. 90357

Lots of glass and soaring ceilings give this house a spacious, contemporary flavor in a compact space. A step down from the front entry, the fireplaced Great room adjoins a convenient kitchen with a sunny breakfast nook. Sliding glass doors open to an angular deck. Three bedrooms, located at the rear of the house, offer protection from street sounds, include a luxurious, vaulted master suite with private bath.

Main living area — 1,368 sq. ft.
Garage — 2-car

Total living area — 1,368 sq. ft.

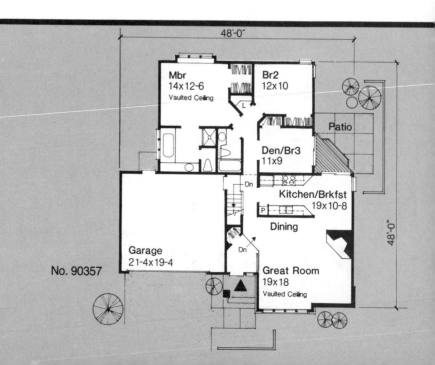

No. 90357

Luxurious Master Suite

No. 90329

On the second floor, the roomy master bedroom with its luxurious master bath and dressing area will be a constant delight. Just a step down from the bedroom itself, the bath incorporates an oversized corner tub, a shower, a walk-in closet, and a skylight. The third bedroom could serve as a loft or sitting room. The open staircase spirals down to the first floor Great room with its vaulted ceiling, fireplace, and corner of windows. The adjacent dining room has a wetbar and direct access to the large, eat-in kitchen. Additional living space is provided by the family room which opens onto the deck through sliding glass doors.

Main floor — 904 sq. ft.
Upper floor — 797 sq. ft.
Basement — 904 sq. ft.
Garage — 405 sq. ft.

Total living area — 1,701 sq. ft.

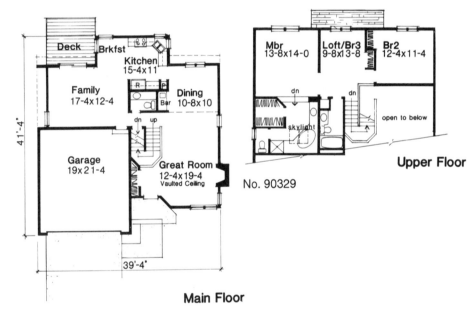

No. 90329

Main Floor

Upper Floor

Striking, Notable, Impressive

No. 91670

What a house! One of our most popular designs ever. This exciting French Contemporary exterior conceals a simple building form — Four bedrooms with two full baths on the upper level and a second stairway to the bonus room. The first floor not only has a spacious living room right off the foyer, but a formal dining area, kitchen with island and eating nook, and a den. The family room has enough space for two families.

First floor — 1,586 sq. ft.
Upper level — 1,433 sq. ft.
Bonus — 305 sq. ft.
Garage — 632 sq. ft.

Total living area — 3,324 sq. ft.

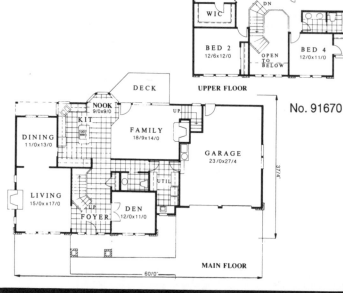

No. 91670

UPPER FLOOR

MASTER 16/6x15/0
SPA
MB
BED3 13/0x13/0
WIC
DN
BONUS 16/6x19/8
BED 2 12/6x12/0
OPEN TO BELOW
BED 4 12/0x11/0

MAIN FLOOR

DECK
NOOK 9/0x9/0
KIT
DINING 11/0x13/0
FAMILY 18/9x14/0
UP
GARAGE 23/0x27/4
UTIL
LIVING 15/0x17/0
FOYER
DEN 12/0x11/0
37'4"
60'0"

Open Plan Features Great Room and Exterior Options

No. 90328

With a skylight and a vaulted ceiling, the Great room will welcome family and guests alike. This inviting room also includes a fireplace, sliding door access to the deck and a wetbar. The roomy eat-in kitchen features an efficient U-shaped work area and lots of windows in the dining area. The three bedrooms and two full baths incorporate unusual angled entries so as to make the most of every foot of floor space. The master bedroom combines its bath and dressing area. The third bedroom would make a cozy den or a handy room for guests.

Main living area — 1,400 sq. ft.
Basement — 1,350 sq. ft.
Garage — 374 sq. ft.

Total living area — 1,400 sq. ft.

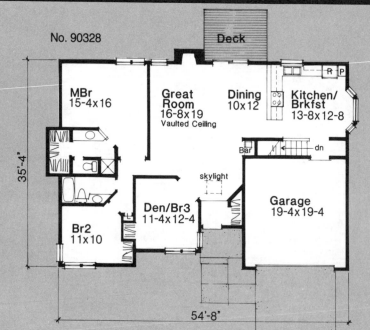

No. 90328

Deck
MBr 15-4x16
Great Room 16-8x19 Vaulted Ceiling
Dining 10x12
Kitchen/ Brkfst 13-8x12-8
Bar
dn
skylight
Den/Br3 11-4x12-4
Garage 19-4x19-4
Br2 11x10
35'-4"
54'-8"

All-American Contemporary

No. 91668

This plan offers up-to-date features of the modern home today. The master suite has a walk-in closet, and a spacious master bath with a whirlpool tub and double vanity. The kitchen features an eating nook that opens into the vaulted family room, which has access to the patio. The dining and living room are set up to make entertaining easy and enjoyable. This plan also offers an innovative loft space with two bedrooms, on the second floor, which are ideal for children.

Main floor — 1,125 sq. ft.
Second floor — 538 sq. ft.
Garage — 420 sq. ft.

Total living area — 1,663 sq. ft.

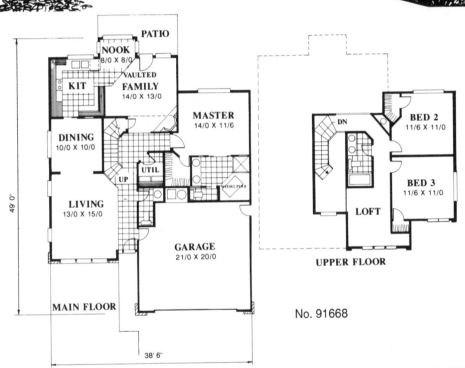

PATIO

NOOK
8/0 X 8/0

KIT

VAULTED
FAMILY
14/0 X 13/0

MASTER
14/0 X 11/6

DINING
10/0 X 10/0

UTIL

UP

WHIRLPOOL

LIVING
13/0 X 15/0

GARAGE
21/0 X 20/0

49' 0"

MAIN FLOOR

38' 6"

DN

BED 2
11/6 X 11/0

BED 3
11/6 X 11/0

LOFT

UPPER FLOOR

No. 91668

A Lot Of House In A Small Package

No. 91674

The modern, efficient kitchen layout of this home is a plus; it is conveniently located off the family room, perfect for entertaining. The island and nook make preparing meals and keeping up with the family conversation at the end of the day easy. The formal dining room runs smoothly into the living room. The master bedroom features a walk-in closet and master bath room. Three other bedrooms, plus a bonus room, are also found on the second floor. This Frank Lloyd Wright inspired contemporary has it all.

First floor — 1,028 sq. ft.
Second floor — 1,043 sq. ft.
Bonus room — 205 sq. ft.
Garage — 390 sq. ft.

Total living area — 2,276 sq. ft.

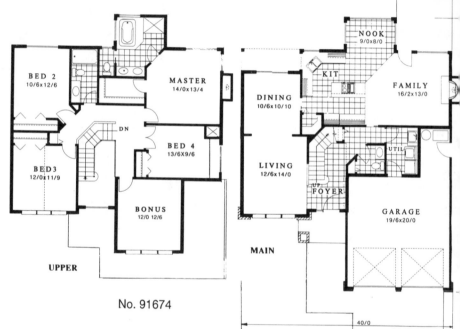

No. 91674

Modern Set-Up

No. 91665

In today's households convenience is the key. This house is convenient. Take the island kitchen for example, pantry space, room for two or more cooks, and it flows freely to the eating nook or the family room. The fireplaced family room is a cozy, relaxing size, and accesses the deck. The formal dining room and fireplaced living room access each other and notice the 13' ceiling height in the living room. The master bedroom has a grand master bath with a walk-in closet. The secondary bedrooms share a bath and have amply closet space.

Main floor — 1,660 sq. ft.
Upper floor — 1,200 sq. ft.
Bonus — 356 sq. ft.

Total living area — 3,216 sq. ft.

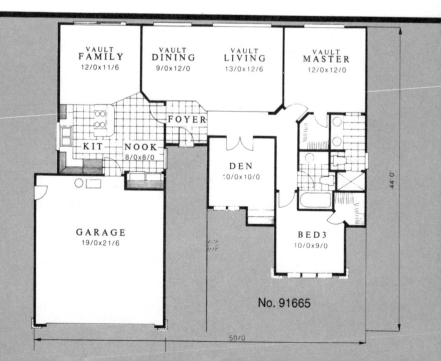

No. 91665

Absolute Design Mastery

No. 91671

This impressive Tudor exterior leads you into a modern 90's floor plan. A flexible vaulted Great room with fireplace, the family and nook are conveniently located off the kitchen — all this and three plus bedrooms are contained in a mere 1,786 sq. ft. The master bedroom features a master bath with a whirlpool tub, double vanity, and walk-in closet.

Main floor — 1,224 sq. ft.
Upper level — 562 sq. ft.
Garage — 400 sq. ft.

Total living area — 1,786 sq. ft.

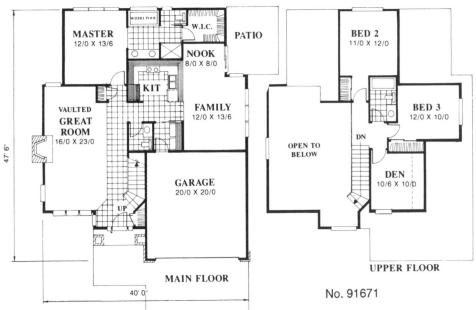

MASTER 12/0 X 13/6
WHIRLPOOL
W.I.C.
PATIO
NOOK 8/0 X 8/0
KIT
FAMILY 12/0 X 13/6
VAULTED GREAT ROOM 16/0 X 23/0
UP
GARAGE 20/0 X 20/0

47' 6"
40' 0"

MAIN FLOOR

BED 2 11/0 X 12/0
BED 3 12/0 X 10/0
OPEN TO BELOW
DN
DEN 10/6 X 10/0

UPPER FLOOR

No. 91671

Luxurious Master Bedroom Suite

No. 90310

The main floor of this contemporary design welcomes guests into the sunken Great room whose vaulted ceiling extends beyond the second floor. In addition to two large windows, it also includes a fireplace with an extended hearth. Just a step up from the Great room is the dining room. A wetbar serves both rooms and is convenient to the efficient U-shaped kitchen. The adjacent breakfast room opens onto the deck and is separated from the kitchen by a serving bar. The master bedroom has an additional, private suite with a fireplace and sliding doors onto the deck. The upper floor is comprised of three more bedrooms; one of which has a private bath, four roof-windows and a walk-in closet.

Main floor — 2,082 sq. ft.
Upper floor — 1,279 sq. ft.
Basement — 2,082 sq. ft.
Garage — 684 sq. ft.

Total living area — 3,361 sq. ft.

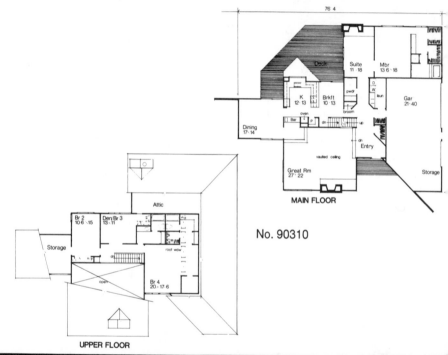

No. 90310

Half-Round Window Graces Attractive Exterior

No. 90395

This handsome home combines convenience and drama by adding a bedroom wing a half-level above active areas. The result of this distinctive design is a striking, spacious feeling in living spaces, along with uncompromised privacy for the two bedrooms at the rear of the house. Look at the soaring ceilings of the kitchen, living, dining, and breakfast rooms. Notice the little touches that make life easier: the private bath entrance from the master suite, the pass-through between kitchen and dining room, the built-in planning desk, the bookcases that flank the fireplace. Don't need a third bedroom? The front room on the entry level doubles as a home office or den.

Main living area — 1,452 sq. ft.
Garage — 2-car

Total living area — 1,452 sq. ft

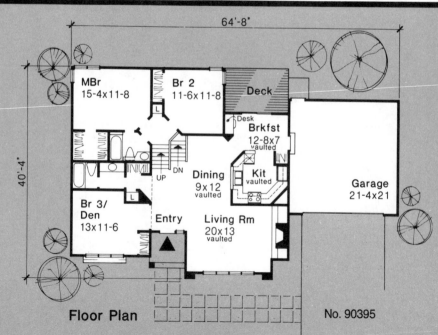

Floor Plan

No. 90395

High Impact Two-Story

No. 99373

Gracious living abounds in this four bedroom upscale 1-1/2 story home, where the family room becomes the focus of intersecting activities. Its high impact effect comes from its two-story entry with double doors and transom. As you enter you see the firplace/window walls of the large two-story family room. The master suite is quite spacious and unique with a curved glass block behind the tub in the master bath. The sitting area in the master suite has a semi-circular window wall and see-thru fireplace, perfect for romantic, cozy evenings. Entertaining is a joy in the gourmet kitchen and breakfast area that opens to a covered lanai. If your guest decides to stay the night, the guest suite is more than accomodating with it's private deck and walk-in closet. The secondary bedrooms share a bath.

Main floor — 3,158 sq. ft.
Upper floor — 1,374 sq. ft.

Total living area — 4,532 sq. ft.

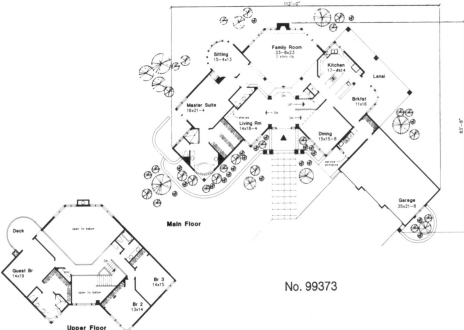

No. 99373

Many Windows Add Eye-Appeal

No. 91638

Stately elegance, within and without, are the hallmarks of this distinctive dwelling. Brick highlights and wide picture windows make this an eye-opener on any street. Behind these windows, on the ground floor, rests a spacious den, hidden away, behind double hardwood doors, and a cozy living room with its own fireplace. Upstairs, from the coved master bedroom the lord and lady of the manor look out upon their domain through their own bright windows, as they contemplate a relaxing interlude in their private spa. Three other bedrooms, plus a large bonus room complete the picture on this floor. With only 2,341 square feet and less than 39 feet deep, there's definitely more to this beauty than meets the eye, and it will be able to find a home on the shallowest lot.

Main floor — 1,181 sq. ft.
Upper floor — 918 sq. ft.
Bonus room — 242 sq. ft.
Garage — 2-car

Total living area — 2,341 sq. ft.

No. 91638

UPPER FLOOR

OPTIONAL UPPER FLOOR

MAIN FLOOR

Single-Level Living

No. 99329

For the move-up or empty-nester buyer who is looking for lots of features, but wants them all on one floor, consider this 1,642 square foot home. The interior offers many surprises like a vaulted ceiling in the living room and a built-in plant shelf. A fireplace forms the focus of this room. The angled kitchen has a sunny breakfast room. The formal dining room has stately divider details. Two bedrooms and two full baths in the sleeping wing of the home include the master suite.

Main living area — 1,642 sq. ft.
Garage — 2-car

Total living area — 1,642 sq. ft.

No. 99329

Floor Plan

With Family In Mind

No. 91666

This plan has modern family living in mind. A very popular plan, this home features an island kitchen which opens up to a spacious family room. The master bedroom is located on the main floor with a walk-in closet and master bath with spa tub. The second floor has two additional bedrooms, full bath, and a bonus room that is a delight for both children and parents. The living room features a fireplace and opens into the dining room for easy entertaining.

Main floor — 1,558 sq. ft.
Second floor — 560 sq. ft.
Bonus room — 280 sq. ft.
Garage — 420 sq. ft.

Total living area — 2,398 sq. ft.

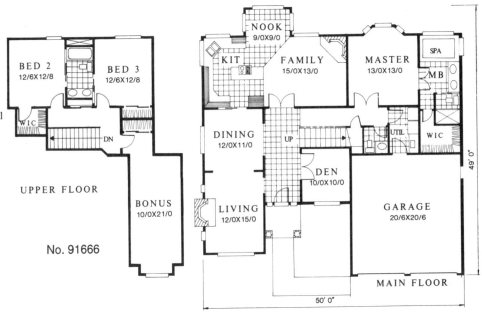

UPPER FLOOR

No. 91666

MAIN FLOOR

Designed With The Sun

No. 99622

This sleek ranch collects and distributes the sun's energy in a form known as passive solar. And, careful design combines open planning with needed privacy. To the right of the central foyer are the kitchen and family room with a heat-circulating fireplace. To the left is the private wing with three big bedrooms and two baths. Concentrated in the dramatic living and dining room space, with sloping ceilings and clerestory windows, are the passive solar elements. A large expanse of glass permits heating of the air and certain interior surfaces. The large stone wall and fireplace assembly stores this heat for times when the sun is not shining. The insulated concrete slab does the same. In addition, the greenhouse builds up heat which is transmitted through another stone wall. Other energy conscious features are also included in this exciting and original design.

Main living area — 1,548 sq. ft.

Garage — 2-car

Total living area — 1,548 sq. ft.

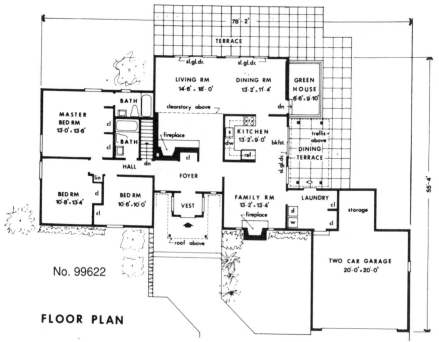

No. 99622

FLOOR PLAN

Elegance in Modern Living

No. 91667

This unbelievable house is the height of elegance, its design features are characteristic of much larger homes. Not only is the main floor a dream come true, but the lower level has a basement large enough for indoor hockey. The voluminous foyer leads you into a coved living room and the kitchen is a chef's delight with its island and eating nook. The master suite features a walk-in closet and master bath with spa tub.

Main floor — 2,830 sq. ft.

Lower level — 1,730 sq. ft.

Garage — 713 sq. ft.

Total living area — 2,830 sq. ft.

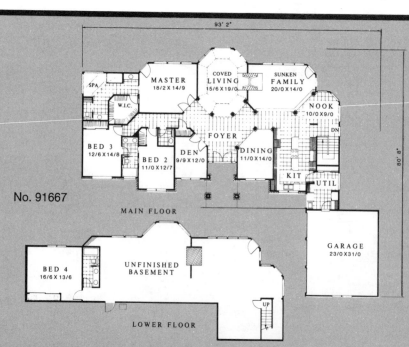

No. 91667

Southwestern Contemporary

No. 91775

This Texas-sized Southwestern contemporary home offers a wide selection of spacious environments. Two colossal columns support a regal, high-gabled porch, creating an elegant entrance portico. Inside, rectangular rooms are clearly in the minority. Only the two bedrooms have four right-angled corners. Interesting angles abound throughout the rest of the plan. The vaulted, sky-lit dining room is octagonal in shape. The parlor and kitchen are modified octagons. The vaulted family room has a fireplace, entertainment center, and sliding glass doors that open onto a formal deck. Kitchen features include a work island with cooktop and grill, and eating bar with an extra sink, built-in ovens, microwave and dishwasher, and a step-in pantry. The eating nook has a high ceiling and sliding glass doors that open onto the patio. This plan also includes a spacious guest suite.

Main living area — 3,600 sq. ft.
Garage — 832 sq. ft.

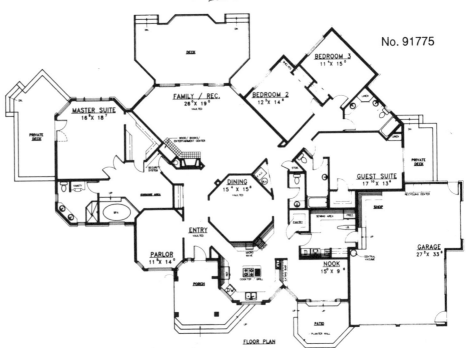

No. 91775

FLOOR PLAN

Total living area — 3,600 sq. ft.

For A Gently Side Sloping Lot

No. 91709

Plans for this four-bedroom home, designed for construction on a gently side-sloping lot, include a three-car garage. Garage and family room are at the lowest level with family living space a half-flight up at mid-level. Sleeping areas are another half-flight up, over the garage and family room. One step down and to the left of the mid-level entryway is a sunken living room. Surrounded by windows, this room is also warmed in winter by a wood stove. The dining room has glass doors that open onto a wide deck. The kitchen features skylights, ample counter space, a work island, pantry, and sunny eating nook. The master bedroom has it's own bath with an oversized walk-in shower stall. A huge linen closet, with extra storage space, is centrally located and a compartmentalized bath with double vanities serves the other three bedrooms.

First floor — 1,539 sq. ft.
Second floor — 1,152 sq. ft.
Garage — 660 sq. ft.

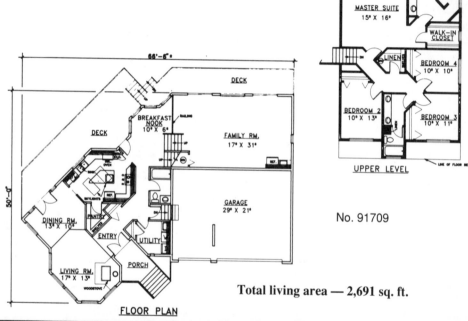

No. 91709

UPPER LEVEL

No. 91709

Total living area — 2,691 sq. ft.

FLOOR PLAN

Skylights Brighten Rooms

No. 92110

A rounded, covered porch leads to an aesthetically pleasing entry with a skylight for extra brightness and an elegant circular staircase. To the right the kitchen features another skylight, plenty of cabinet space, an eat-in nook and exits to an extra-long deck. The sunken, fireplaced living room is flooded with light from sliding glass doors and two large windows. The convenient first-floor laundry room has built-in shelving and ample space for appliances. The master bath offers a skylight, a double vanity, an elegant window seat, his-n-her showers and an enormous walk-in closet. The spacious recreation room with a fireplace has interesting window works and includes easy access to the top deck.

Main living area — 2,314 sq. ft.
Basement area — 1,302 sq. ft.
Garage — 1,017 sq. ft.

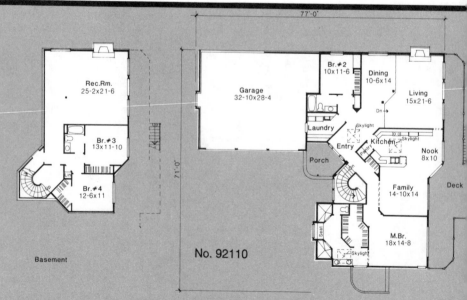

No. 92110

Total living area — 3,616 sq. ft.

Spread-Out Living

No. 91776

The master bedroom anchors one end of the house, the kids' rooms anchor the other. In fact, this home has a demilitarized zone between the teenagers' rumpus rooms and the parents' refuge of two rooms, four walls, and enough linear feet to satisfy any house rule on decibel levels. On the other hand, a retired couple may enjoy the medium size of this home also. It features a formal dining room overlooking a flower garden and a sun-soaked living room. Inside, guests enter a triangle: the family room at the top, dining room to the left, and living room with high ceilings on the right. The master suite has a large walk-in closet and a spa.

Main living area — 1,798 sq. ft.
Garage — 484 sq. ft.

Total living area — 1,798 sq. ft.

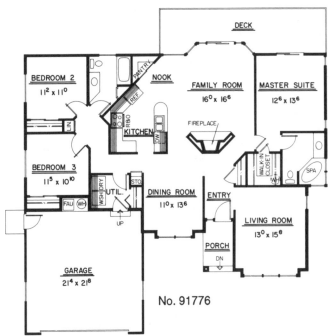

No. 91776

Gable And Glass Grace Facade

No. 91640

A stunning blend of traditional and contemporary styles! Brick, broken gables and what seems to be acres of glass, make this the one all the neighbors will talk about. A unique feature is the sun room that opens directly into the family room as well as to the cavernous three-car garage. A modern wrap-around kitchen with central island commands the ground floor, with easy access to the dining room and living room, via the wide-open, spacious foyer which leads up a wide stairway to the upper floor with its imposing master suite, three other bedrooms and a bonus room.

Main floor — 1,540 sq. ft.
Upper floor — 1,178 sq. ft.
Bonus room — 222 sq. ft.

Total living area — 2,940 sq. ft.

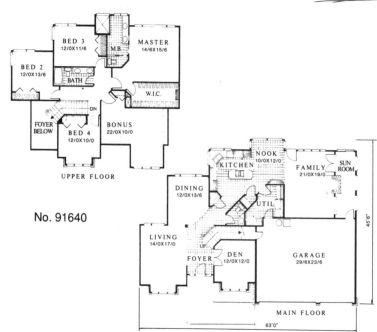

No. 91640

The Most House For Your Building Dollar

No. 91672

This plan works for growing families, empty-nesters, and single folk. With every turn there is drama and function. Notice the upper floor economically tucked under the roof line. The great hall leads into the island kitchen with eating nook. The family room and living room both feature a fireplace. The master bedroom features a walk-in closet and master bath with spa tub. The two additional bedrooms upstairs feature walk-in closets, and share a full bath.

Main floor — 1,928 sq. ft.
Upper floor — 504 sq. ft.
Bonus room — 335 sq. ft.
Garage — 440 sq. ft.

Total living area — 2,432 sq. ft.

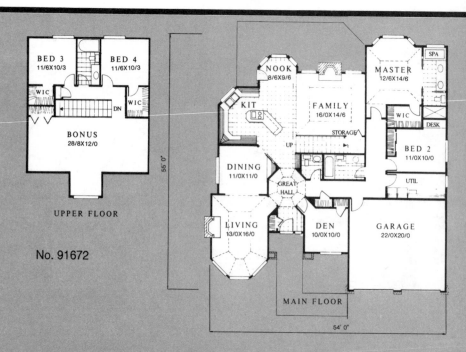

No. 91672

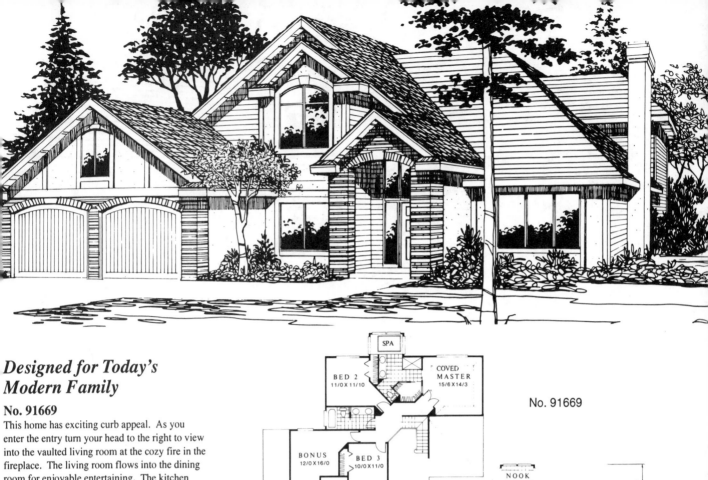

Designed for Today's Modern Family

No. 91669

This home has exciting curb appeal. As you enter the entry turn your head to the right to view into the vaulted living room at the cozy fire in the fireplace. The living room flows into the dining room for enjoyable entertaining. The kitchen features an island and an eating nook. The family room, usually the hub of family life, also has a fireplace. Upstairs the coved master bedroom features a walk-in closet and a master bath with spa tub. The two additional bedrooms share a full bath.

Main floor — 1,200 sq. ft.
Upper floor — 917 sq. ft.
Bonus — 230 sq. ft.
Garage — 462 sq. ft.

Total living area — 2,347 sq. ft.

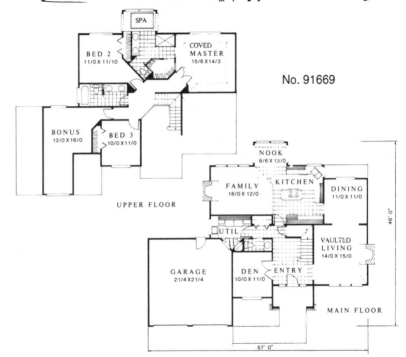

No. 91669

SPA

BED 2
11/0 X 11/10

COVED MASTER
15/6 X 14/3

BONUS
12/0 X 16/0

BED 3
10/0 X 11/0

UPPER FLOOR

NOOK
8/6 X 12/0

FAMILY
16/0 X 12/0

KITCHEN

DINING
11/0 X 11/0

UTIL

VAULTED LIVING
14/0 X 15/0

GARAGE
21/4 X 21/4

DEN
10/0 X 11/0

ENTRY

46' 0"

57' 0"

MAIN FLOOR

Bright and Beautiful

No. 91629

Here's a handsome home with a sunny
atmosphere that comes from towering windows,
rear-facing glass walls, and an open plan. Step
down from the central foyer to a spacious living
and dining room arrangement warmed by a
fireplace and a floor-to-ceiling window. Or step
down to the central hallway that leads past the
den, utility areas and powder room to informal
areas at the rear of the house. Another fireplace
keeps the family room, nook, and kitchen
temperate even on the coldest day. And when the
weather's warm, throw open the door to the patio
and enjoy the outdoor atmosphere. Upstairs,
you'll find three bedrooms, two full baths, and an
unfinished bonus room with a huge, bump-out
window.

First floor — 1,249 sq. ft.
Second floor — 878 sq. ft.
Bonus room — 244 sq. ft.
Garage — 2-car

Total living area —2,127 sq. ft.

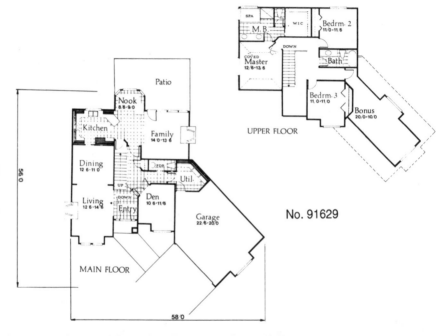

No. 91629

Interesting Angles for One-Floor Living

No. 20193

The house has a dramatic entrance foyer with ten-
foot ceilings in the dining room and living room.
The kitchen is a unique wrap-around shape and
leads into a diamond-shaped breakfast area which
overlooks a deck. The master bedroom suite
includes a decorative ceiling and has lots of
privacy because the other two bedrooms are at
the opposite side of the house with their own
bathroom. The house has many extras such as
skylights and built-in shelves in the closets. This
house is full of unique surprises.

Main living area — 2,250 sq. ft.
Basement — 2,291 sq. ft.
Garage — 573 sq. ft.

Total living area — 2,250 sq. ft.

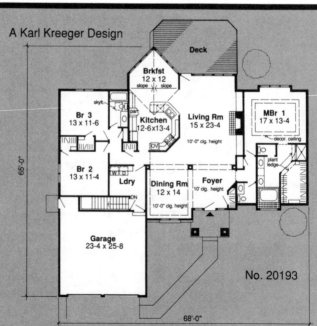

A Karl Kreeger Design

No. 20193

Impressive Comtemporary

No. 91673

Keeping up with the Jones'! You can't miss with this completely functional, completely impressive home. It lacks nothing! The master bedroom has a coved ceiling and features a master bath with double sink vanity, spa and walk-in closet. There is also, a good sized bonus room for storage or extra living space. The modern kitchen features an eating nook but also flows easily into a formal dining room. The family room features a fireplace. The living room is a nice size and there is even a den. Dynamite in a small package.

Main floor — 1,007 sq. ft.
Upper floor — 763 sq. ft.
Bonus room — 280 sq. ft.
Garage — 616 sq. ft.

Total living area — 2,074 sq. ft.

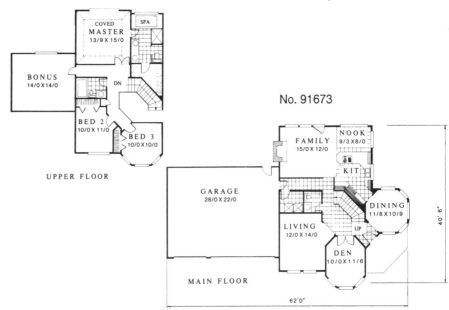

No. 91673

COVED
MASTER
13/9 X 15/0

SPA

BONUS
14/0 X 14/0

DN

BED 2
10/0 X 11/0

BED 3
10/0 X 10/0

UPPER FLOOR

FAMILY
15/0 X 12/0

NOOK
9/3 X 8/0

KIT

GARAGE
28/0 X 22/0

DINING
11/8 X 10/9

LIVING
12/0 X 14/0

UP

DEN
10/0 X 11/6

MAIN FLOOR

40' 6"

62'0"

Four-Bedroom Contemporary

No. 20527

Architectural treatments such as curved walls and beams express the structure of this contemporary home and provide it with great visual appeal. It is designed with innovative ideas that emphasize comfort and the desire for open space. A central hall with a two-story foyer creates an excellent circulation flow and opens the house to a great living and dining area. A comfortable kitchen connects the dinette and family room for informal everyday activities. A powder room and ample closet space on the main floor make this home the perfect answer for today's busy family. Upstairs, a set of skylights brighten the second floor hallway which serves four bedrooms and two full baths. The master suite features an elegant and spacious bathroom with all the closet space you ever dreamed of, including a dressing area.

First floor — 962 sq. ft.
Second floor — 930 sq. ft.
Garage/mudroom — 509 sq. ft.
Optional basement — 874 sq. ft.

No. 20527

Total living area — 1,892 sq. ft.

Bedrooms, Game Room Crown Design

No. 22002

Heavily glassed and airy, the upper level of this two-story contemporary includes two large bedrooms plus a 15-ft. game room with adjoining balcony. Below, another game room and separate family room with a fireplace allow for the many activities of a large family. A dining room and a kitchen with additional dining space are featured, and the master bedroom adjoins its own opulent bath complex.

First floor — 2,456 sq. ft.
Second floor — 728 sq. ft.
Garage — 495 sq. ft.

Total living area —3,184 sq. ft.

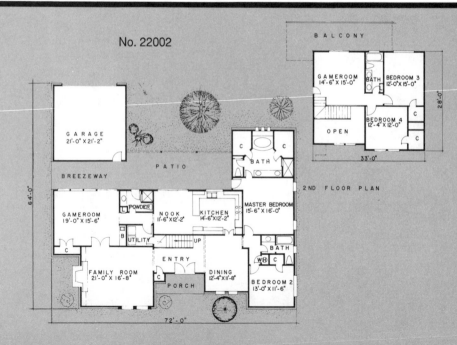

No. 22002

Contemporary Drama

No. 20450

Here's a practical home loaded with drama and charm. The glass wall over the front door provides an impressive introduction to this exciting contemporary designed with handicapped access in mind. Living and dining rooms, divided by a two-way fireplace, soar to dizzying heights. You'll love the easy-care arrangement of the kitchen and breakfast room overlooking the curved porch. The rear bedroom nearby features a full wall of closets and private access to a full bath. Walk up the central staircase to three angular bedrooms, each with a gabled window seat, and a spectacular, second-floor deck. You'll find built-in desks in the kids' rooms, and the master suite boasts a luxury bath, abundant closet space, and an adjoining office.

First floor — 1,412 sq. ft.
Second floor — 1,292 sq. ft.
Basement — 1,412 sq. ft.
Porch — 190 sq. ft.
Garage — 620 sq. ft.

Total living area — 2,704 sq. ft.

No. 20450

Second Floor

Deck

Br 2
12 x 11-1

desk
desk

Br 3
12 x 11-1

MBr 1
15-8 x 15-2

DN

lin.
lin.

slope

open to below

Office/Storage
15-8 x 11-8

First Floor

Porch
12 x 15-6

Br 4
14-6 x 13

Brkfst
12 x 11

Kit
11-6 x 13-8

ramp

DN

lin.

Dining Rm
15-6 x 11

shelves

Garage
23-6 x 25-8

UP

Living Rm
15-6 x 15-6

Foyer

slope

44'-0"

48'-0"

Everything you need to make your dream come true!

You pay only a fraction of the original cost for home designs by respected professionals.

You've picked your dream home!

You can already see it standing on your lot... you can see yourselves in your new home... enjoying family, entertaining guests, celebrating holidays. All that remains ahead are the details. That's where we can help.

Whether you plan to build-it-yourself, be your own contractor, or hand your plans over to an outside contractor, your Garlinghouse blueprints provide the perfect beginning for putting yourself in your dream home right away.

We even make it simple for you to make professional design modifications. We can also provide a materials list for greater economy.

My grandfather, L.F. Garlinghouse, started a tradition of quality when he founded this company in 1907. For over 85 years, homeowners and builders have relied on us for accurate, complete, professional blueprints. Our plans help you get results fast... and save money, too! These pages will give you all the information you need to order. So get started now... I know you'll love your new Garlinghouse home!

Sincerely,

Here's What You Get!

1 Exterior Elevations

Exact scale views of the front, rear, and both sides of your home, showing exterior materials, details, and all necessary measurements.

2 Detailed Floor Plans

Showing the placement of all interior walls, the dimensions of rooms, doors, windows, stairways, and other details.

3 Foundation Plan

With footings and all load-bearing points as applicable to your home, including all necessary notations and dimensions. The foundation style supplied varies from home to home. Local conditions and practices will determine whether a basement, crawl-space, or a slab is best for you. Your professional contractor can easily make the necessary adaption.

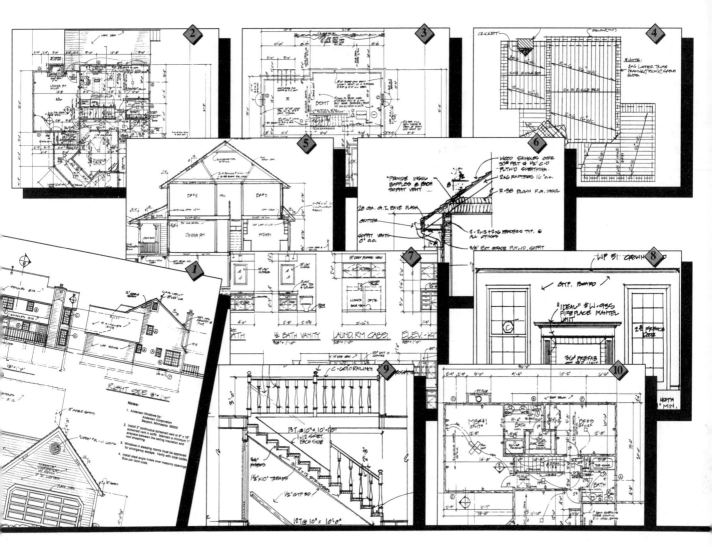

4 Roof Plan

All information necessary to construct the roof for your home is included. Many blueprints contain framing plans showing all of the roof elements, so you'll know how these details look and fit together.

5 Typical Cross-Section

A detailed, full cross-sectional view through the entire house, as if the house was cut from top to bottom. This elevation allows a contractor to better understand the interconnections of the construction components.

6 Typical Wall Sections

Detailed views of your exterior wall, as though sliced from top to bottom. These drawings clarify exterior wall construction, insulation, flooring, and roofing details. Depending on your specific geography and climate, your home will be built with either 2x4 or 2x6 exterior walls. Most professional contractors can easily adapt plans for either requirement.

7 Kitchen & Bath Cabinet Details

These plans or, in some cases, elevations show the specific details and placement of the cabinets in your kitchen and bathrooms, as applicable. Customizing these areas is simpler beginning with these details.

8 Fireplace Details

When your home includes one or more fireplaces, these detailed drawings will help your mason with their construction and appearance. It is easy to review details with professionals when you have the plans for reference.

9 Stair Details

If stairs are part of the design you selected, specific plans are included for their construction and details.

10 Schematic Electrical Layouts

The suggested locations for all of your switches, outlets, and fixtures are indicated on these drawings. They are practical as they are, but they are also a solid taking-off point for any personal adaptions.

Also available, is a money-saving Materials List.

Plus...

FREE

Specifications and Contract Form

FREE

14-page Energy Conservation Guide.

TURN THE PAGE FOR THE EASY STEPS TO COMPLETE YOUR DREAM HOME ORDER!

Garlinghouse options and extras make the dream truly yours.

Reversed Plans Can Make Your Dream Home Just Right!

"That's our dream home... if only the garage were on the other side!"

You could have exactly the home you want by flipping it end-for-end. Check it out by holding your dream home page of this book up to a mirror. Then simply order your plans "reversed". We'll send you one full set of mirror-image plans (with the writing backwards) as a master guide for you and your builder.

The remaining sets of your order will come as shown in this book so the dimensions and specifications are easily read on the job site... but they will be specially stamped "REVERSED" so there is no construction confusion.

We can only send reversed plans with multiple-set orders. But, there is no extra charge for this service.

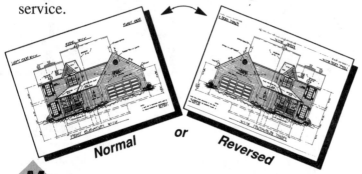

Normal   or   Reversed

Modifying Your Garlinghouse Home Plan

Easy modifications to your dream home... minor non-structural changes, simple materials substitutions... can be made between you and your builder.

However, if you are considering making major changes to your design, we strongly recommend that you use an architect or a professional designer. And, since you have already started with our complete detailed blueprints, the cost of those expensive professional services will be significantly less.

Our Reproducible Vellums Make Modifications Easier

They provide a design professional with the right way to make changes directly to your Garlinghouse home plans and then print as many copies of the modified plans as you need. The price is $395 plus shipping. Call 1-800-235-5700 to find out more.

Remember To Order Your Materials List

It'll help you save money. Available at a modest additional charge, the Materials List gives the quantity, dimensions, and specifications for the major materials needed to build your home. You will get faster, more accurate bids from your contractors and building suppliers — and avoid paying for unused materials and waste. Materials Lists are available for all home plans except as otherwise indicated, but can only be ordered with a set of home plans. Due to differences in local building codes, regional requirements, and homeowner/builder preferences... electrical, plumbing & heating/air conditioning equipment requirements aren't provided.

How Many Sets Of Plans Will You Need?

The Standard 8-Set Construction Package

Our experience shows that you'll speed every step of construction and avoid costly building errors by ordering enough sets to go around. Each tradesperson wants a set — the general contractor and all subcontractors; foundation, electrical, plumbing, heating/air conditioning, drywall, finish carpenters, and cabinet shop. Don't forget your lending institution, building deparament and, of course, a set for yourself.

The Minimum 5-Set Construction Package

If you're comfortable with arduous follow-up, this package can save you a few dollars. You might have enough copies to go around if work goes exactly as scheduled and no plans are lost or damaged. But for only $30 more, the 8-set package eliminates these worries.

The Single-Set Decision-Maker Package

We offer this set so you can study the blueprints to plan your dream home in detail. But remember... one set is never enough to build your home... and they're copyrighted.

Questions?

Call our customer service number at 1-203-632-0500.
An important note:

All plans are drawn to conform to one or more of the industry's major national building standards. However, due to the variety of local building regulations, your plan may need to be modified to comply with local requirements — snow loads, energy loads, seismic zones, etc. Do check them fully and consult your local building officials.

A few states require that all building plans used be drawn by an architect registered in that state. While having your plans reviewed and stamped by such an architect may be prudent, laws requiring non-conforming plans like ours to be completely redrawn forces you to unnecessarily pay very large fees. If your state has such a law, we strongly recommend you contact your state representative to protest.

Important Shipping Information

Your order is processed immediately. Allow 10 working days from our receipt of your order for normal UPS delivery. Save time with your credit card and our "800" number. UPS *must* have a street address or Rural Route Box number — never a post office box. Use a work address if no one is home during the day.

Orders being shipped to Alaska, Hawaii, APO, FPO or Post Office Boxes must go via First Class Mail. Please include the proper postage.

Canadian Orders and Shipping:

To our friends in Canada, we have a plan design affiliate in Kitchener, Ontario. This relationship will help you avoid the delays and charges associated with shipments from the United States. Morever, our affiliate is familiar with the building requirements in your community and country.

We prefer payments in U.S. Currency. If you, however, are sending Canadian funds, please add 30% to the prices of the plans and shipping fees.

Domestic Shipping (stated in U.S. dollars)		
UPS Ground Service		$ 7.00
First Class Mail		$ 8.50
Express Delivery Service Call For Details 1-800-235-5700		
International Shipping (stated in U.S. dollars)		
	One Set	**Mult. Sets**
Canada	$7.25	$ 12.50
All Other Nations	$18.50	$50.00

Canadian Orders are now Duty Free

Please submit all Canadian plan orders to:
The Garlinghouse Company, Inc.
20 Cedar Street North
Kitchener, Ontario N2H, 2W8
Canadian orders only: 1-800-561-4169
Fax #: 1-519-743-1282
Customer Service #: 1-519-743-4169

Mexico and Other Countries:

If you are ordering from outside the United States, please note that your check, money order, or international money transfer **must be payable in U.S. currency.** For speed, we ship international orders Air Parcel Post. Please refer to the chart for the correct shipping cost.

Blueprint Price Schedule (stated in U.S. dollars)	
Standard Constuction Package (8 sets)	$255.00
Minimum Construction Package (5 sets)	225.00
Single-Set Package (no reverses)	180.00
Each Additional Set (ordered w/one above)	20.00
Materials List (with plan order only)	25.00

ORDER TOLL FREE — 1-800-235-5700

Monday-Friday 8:00am to 5:00pm Eastern Time
or FAX your Credit Card order to (203)632-0712
All other nations
call 1-203-632-0500. Please have the following at your fingertips before you call:

1. *Your credit card number*
2. *The plan number*
3. *The order code number*

Blueprint Order Form   Order Code #H3MD1

Prices subject to change without notice.

Plan No. _____

❑ As Shown   ❑ Reversed *(mult. set pkgs. only)*

	Each	Amount
8 set pkg.	$255.00	$
5 set pkg.	$225.00	$
1 set pkg.*(no reverses)*	$180.00	$
__(Qty.) Add. sets @	$ 20.00	$
Material List	$ 25.00	$
Shipping — see chart		$
Subtotal		$
Sales Tax (CT residents add 6% sales tax, KS residents add 5.9% sales tax)		$
Total Amount Enclosed		$

Thank you for your order!

Send your check, money order or credit card information to:
Garlinghouse Company
34 Industrial Park Place, P.O. Box 1717
Middletown, CT 06457

Bill To: *(address must be as it appears on credit card statement)*

Name _____
(Please Print)

Address _____

City/State _____ Zip _____

Daytime Phone ( ) _____

Ship To *(if different from Bill to):*

Name _____

Address _____
(UPS will not ship to P.O. Boxes)

City/State _____ Zip _____

Credit Card Information

Charge To: ❑ Mastercard ❑ Visa ❑ Discover

Card #|__|__|__|__|__|__|__|__|__|__|__|__|__|__|__|__|

Signature _____ Exp. ___/___

GARAGE PLANS

Save money by Doing-It-Yourself using our Easy-To-Follow plans. Whether you intend to build your own garage or contract it out to a building professional, the Garlinghouse garage plans provide you with everything you need to price out your project and get started. Put our 85 years of experience to work for you.
Order now!!

ITEM NO. 06016C — $86.00
Apartment Garage With One Bedroom

- 24' x 28' Overall Dimensions
- 544 Square Foot Apartment
- 12/12 Gable Roof with Dormers
- Slab or Stem Wall Foundation Options

ITEM NO. 06015C — $86.00
Apartment Garage With Two Bedrooms

- 26' x 28' Overall Dimensions
- 728 Square Foot Apartment
- 4/12 Pitch Gable Roof
- Slab or Stem Wall Foundation Options

ITEM NO. 06012C — $54.00
30' Deep Gable &/or Eave Jumbo Garages

- 4/12 Pitch Gable Roof
- Available Options for Extra Tall Walls, Garage & Personnel Doors, Foundation, Window, & Sidings
- Package contains 4 Different Sizes
  - 30' x 28' • 30' x 32' • 30' x 36' • 30' x 40'

ITEM NO. 06013C — $68.00
Two-Car Garage With Mudroom/Breezeway

- Attaches to Any House
- 24' x 24' Eave Entry
- Available Options for Utility Room with Bath, Mudroom, Screened-In Breezeway, Roof, Foundation, Garage & Personnel Doors, Window, & Sidings

ITEM NO. 06001C — $48.00
12', 14', & 16' Wide-Gable 1-Car Garages

- Available Options for Roof, Foundation, Window, Door, & Sidings
- Package contains 8 Different Sizes
- 12' x 20' Mini-Garage ● 14' x 22' ● 16' x 20' ● 16' x 24'
- 14' x 20'   ● 14' x 24' ● 16' x 22' ● 16' x 26'

ITEM NO. 06003C — $48.00
24' Wide-Gable 2-Car Garages

- Available Options for Side Shed, Roof, Foundation, Garage & Personnel Doors, Window, & Sidings
- Package contains 5 Different Sizes
- 24' x 22'   ● 24' x 24'   ● 24' x 26'
- 24' x 28'   ● 24' x 32'

ITEM NO. 06007C — $60.00
Gable 2-Car Gambrel Roof Garages

- Interior Rear Stairs to Loft Workshop
- Front Loft Cargo Door With Pulley Lift
- Available Options for Foundation, Garage & Personnel Doors, Window, & Sidings
- Package contains 5 Different Sizes
- 22' x 26' ● 22' x 28' ● 24' x 28' ● 24' x 30' ● 24' x 32'

ITEM NO. 06006C — $48.00
22' & 24' Deep Eave 2 & 3-Car Garages

- Can Be Built Stand-Alone or Attached to House
- Available Options for Roof, Foundation, Garage & Personnel Doors, Window, & Sidings
- Package contains 6 Different Sizes
- 22' x 28'   ● 22' x 32'   ● 24' x 32'
- 22' x 30'   ● 24' x 30'   ● 24' x 36'

ITEM NO. 06002C — $48.00
20' & 22' Wide-Gable 2-Car Garages

- Available Options for Roof, Foundation, Garage & Personnel Doors, Window, & Sidings
- Package contains 7 Different Sizes
- 20' x 20'   ● 20' x 24'   ● 22' x 22'   ● 22' x 28'
- 20' x 22'   ● 20' x 28'   ● 22' x 24'

ITEM NO. 06008C — $60.00
Eave 2 & 3-Car Clerestory Roof Garages

- Interior Side Stairs to Loft Workshop
- Available Options for Engine Lift, Foundation, Garage & Personnel Doors, Window, & Sidings
- Package contains 4 Different Sizes
- 24' x 26'   ● 24' x 28'   ● 24' x 32'   ● 24' x 36'

Here's What You Get

- Three complete sets of drawings for each plan ordered.
- Detailed step-by-step instructions with easy-to-follow diagrams on how to build your garage (not available with apartment/garages).
- For each garage style, a variety of size and garage door configuration options.
- Variety of roof styles and/or pitch options for most garages.

- Complete materials list.
- Choice between three foundation options: Monolithic Slab, Concrete Stem Wall or Concrete Block Stem Wall.
- Full framing plans, elevations and cross-sectionals for each garage size and configuration.
- And Much More!!

Order Information For Garage Plans:

All garage plan orders contain three complete sets of drawings with instructions and are priced as listed next to the illustration. Additional sets of plans may be obtained for $10.00 each with your original order. UPS shipping is used unless otherwise requested. Please include the proper amount for shipping.

GARLINGHOUSE

Build-It-Yourself PROJECT PLAN

Garage Order Form

Please send me 3 complete sets of the following GARAGE PLAN:

Item no. & description	Price
_____	$ _____
Additional Sets	
_____ (@ $10.00 each)	$ _____
Shipping Charges: UPS-$3.75, First Class- $4.50	$ _____
Subtotal:	$ _____
Resident sales tax: KS-5.9%, CT-6%	$ _____
Total Enclosed:	$ _____

Send your order to:
(With check or money order payable in U.S. funds only)
The Garlinghouse Company
34 Industrial Park Place
P.O. Box 1717
Middletown, CT 06457

No C.O.D. orders accepted; U.S. funds only. UPS will not ship to Post Office boxes, FPO boxes, APO boxes, Alaska or Hawaii. Canadian orders must be shipped First Class.

Prices subject to change without notice.

Order Code No. **G3MD1**

My Billing Address is:
Name _____
Address _____
City _____
State _____ Zip _____
Daytime Phone No. _____

My Shipping Address is:
Name _____
Address _____
(UPS will not ship to P.O. Boxes)
City _____
State _____ Zip _____

For Faster Service...Charge It!
U.S. & Canada Call
1(800)235-5700
All foreign residents call 1(203)632-0500
❏ Mastercard ❏ Visa ❏ Discover

Card # | | | | | | | | | | | | | | | | | | | |

Signature _____ Exp.___ / ___

If paying by credit card, to avoid delays:
billing address must be as it appears on credit card statement
or FAX us at (203) 632-0712